A PRAEGER WORLD OF ART PROFILE

HENRY MOORE

HENRY MOORE

A study of his life and work

HERBERT READ

FREDERICK A. PRAEGER, Publishers
NEW YORK • WASHINGTON

BOOKS THAT MATTER

PUBLISHED IN THE UNITED STATES OF AMERICA IN 1966
BY FREDERICK A. PRAEGER, INC., PUBLISHERS
111 FOURTH AVENUE, NEW YORK, N.Y. 10003
SECOND PRINTING, 1967
ALL RIGHTS RESERVED

Contents

Preface

The purpose of this book is to tell the story of Henry Moore's life, which, after his childhood and early education, is mainly the story of his art. I have had the privilege, not only of a long and close friendship with the artist, but also of his cooperation in this enterprise. While I do not wish to hold him responsible for any of the facts presented, much less for the interpretation I have given of his works, nevertheless Henry Moore has read my manuscript and where necessary made corrections. He did not take exception to any of my speculations.

Apart from this essential cooperation, my task was made much easier by the fact that Henry Moore is himself the best photographer of his sculpture. Practically all the illustrations in the volume are reproduced from prints he has supplied to the publisher. Again, he was not responsible for the choice of pieces to be illustrated, nor for their arrangement in the volume. With a few exceptions, all the works discussed in the text are also illustrated. In the case of these exceptions, references are given to the plates in the three-volume *catalogue raisonné* of Moore's work (see Bibliography). The plates in these volumes are indicated by the abbreviation LH I, II and III, followed by the number of the plate.

In all practical matters I have had the tireless assistance of the publisher's editor, Miss Patricia Lowman. I would also like to thank my daughter, Mrs Nicholas Hare, who was responsible for the faultless typing of my manuscript.

H.R.

*2 Henry Moore working on
Reclining Figure, 1959–64*

Part One

LIFE

4 Henry Moore, aged 11

CHAPTER ONE

Origins and Early Environment

Henry Moore was born at Castleford in the West Riding of York-shire on 30 July 1898. He was the seventh child of Raymond Spencer Moore, a coal-miner, and of Mary Baker his wife, who came from Staffordshire. Spencer was the name of the father's mother, and Raymond Spencer Moore was so proud of it that he gave it as a second name to all his children, girls as well as boys. He was born in the neighbouring county of Lincolnshire, and according to the family tradition his grandfather, the great-grandfather of Henry, was of Irish origin and worked on the land. It is not known whether he was an immigrant, but it was the period of excess population and famine in Ireland, so this is more than likely.

Both Henry's parents were individuals of strong and independent character. His father, who was born in 1849 and died in 1921, had attended a rural school until he went to work at the age of nine, earning a few pence a week for scaring crows. It is not known at what age he left the land and moved to Castleford to work in the pits, but it was quite early in his life. He was a man of natural intelligence and innate sensibility. He taught himself to play the violin, and one of his early ambitions was that Henry should learn the instrument professionally. He made his son take lessons, but Henry loathed it—he could not bear the aching of his wrist and the horrible noise he made. But he had to persist until he had twice failed an exami-nation, and then his father shifted his interest to the homework Henry brought from school. He helped Henry with his geometry and algebra, and with the reading of Shakespeare, subjects which he had studied from the autodidactic textbooks available in those days. His self-education had also been directed towards improving his position in the mines. Eventually he passed the examinations that qualified him to become first a 'deputy' and then an 'under-manager', but he was never to occupy this second position because his eyes were injured in a pit accident and he was disqualified from further work underground.

The Yorkshire miners of this time were a class apart, proud of their dangerous and skilful calling, anxious to improve their social and cultural conditions. Raymond Moore was a personal friend of Herbert Smith, who lived in the same street in Castleford, and it was Smith who had organized the Yorkshire miners into a trade union and had become their first president. Henry can remember the meetings and discussions that sometimes took place in the 'front-room' of their house.

Henry's mother was equally exceptional in her character and determination. Raymond Coxon's portrait of her *(Pl. 6)* is an eloquent witness to these qualities. She brought up a large family of

5 Raymond Spencer Moore, 1871

6 Mary Moore, the artist's mother. Portrait by Raymond Coxon, c. 1927

eight children (there was a sister, Elsie, who was born later than Henry), and in addition, in times of stress, she would go out to work. Henry remembers a strike of the Yorkshire miners which happened when he was about seven or eight and which went on for nearly two years. During this period Mrs Moore worked for a family called Clokie, who owned a pottery in Castleford, and Henry would sometimes go with her and be invited to stay to tea. During this same long period of unemployment the father bought an iron last and began to mend shoes, first for his numerous family, and then, in order to earn a little, for their neighbours.

Of Henry's seven brothers and sisters only five survived into adult life. One, William, died in his first year, and Elsie died when Henry was about fifteen. Of all the family she was nearest to Henry and her death, under rather tragic circumstances, deeply affected him. Unknown to him she had a weak heart, but at the same time had a passion for swimming, at which sport she became very proficient and won several prizes at the new Public Baths that were opened about 1911. But she over-strained her weak heart and died, and Henry always remembered guiltily how he had often encouraged her to run and race with him.

The eldest child of the family was a girl, Annie, who married and had a large family and very many grand- and great-grand-children. The eldest brother, Raymond, came next; after a schooling in Castleford he went to York Training College and qualified as a teacher. A second brother, Alfred, went to Canada when Henry was still at school and was lost to sight. The fourth child, Willie, died in infancy. Next was another sister, Mary, who, like her brother Raymond, became a teacher. A third sister, Elizabeth, also in her turn became a teacher and afterwards married a schoolmaster. A certain pattern thus prevailed in the family—the parents were ambitious for their children, two of whom rose to the top of the teaching profession, whilst another married a man who became a headmaster. When the father's health began to fail, which was about 1920, Mary applied for a country post and became headmistress of a village school at Wighton in Norfolk. Her parents came to live with her in the schoolhouse and thus the family lost all connection with mining and the industrial landscape of the North, though Henry, as we shall see, returned after his service in the First World War to continue his education there.

The industrial landscape of Henry's childhood, or rather townscape, should now be described because it undoubtedly had a formative influence on his future development. Castleford itself is a small town on the eastern edge of the industrial region which occupies most of the southern part of the West Riding of Yorkshire. When the Moores lived there its population was about 20,000; up to 1841 it had been less than 2,000, but it expanded rapidly during

7 Castleford, Yorkshire, a general view

the second half of the nineteenth century. To the north and west
are situated the larger industrial cities of Wakefield and Leeds; to
the north and east is the ancient city of York, and not far beyond all
these cities, about thirty miles to the north-east and north-west of
Castleford, stretch the Yorkshire dales and moors, wild romantic
scenery rich in the sites and ruins of Roman camps and medieval
monasteries. But the immediate environs of Castleford are not un-
interesting. 'Within a radius of some few miles from the town',
relates the local historian, 'we have ancient earthworks, the ruins of
a feudal castle, the sites of famous battlefields, quaint old manor
houses, and the seats of families who have taken an active part in
the stirring events of their time'.[1]

There was nothing romantic about Castleford itself—it was, and
still is, a typical product of the industrial revolution. Built for the
most part of red brick, it has no single feature to distinguish it from
any other town of its size in the mining districts of Northern England.
Even the church, which in most towns in the district preserves some

ancient architectural features, was so thoroughly reconstructed in 1866 that nothing of interest remains. A few relics of the Roman occupation have been discovered, a milestone (for Castleford was on Watling Street, the Roman road to the North), an altar, and numerous burial urns. But these relics have not been preserved in the town itself, but sent to museums in cities like Leeds.

A Mechanics Hall was founded in 1859, later to become the Free Library, and the town boasts a park, the Queen's Park, of thirteen acres. These were the only cultural amenities in a community dedicated to the mining of coal and the manufacture of glass bottles and earthenware jars. It is true that the local potteries used to make cream-coloured pottery known as Queen's Ware, decorated with transfer-prints, but even this was an inferior imitation of the similar pottery made at Leeds which had some distinction of quality and design. More attractive, to a visually sensitive child, were the wares of great variety displayed in the covered market in the centre of the town. Even today this market, with its open booths piled up with rolls of printed cloth, hanging carpets, garish jewellery and heaps of bright oranges and apples has something of the appearance and fascination of an oriental bazaar.

It would be a mistake to regard such a physical environment as in any sense frustrating to a boy like Henry at the beginning of this century. He himself now declares that he would not change his childhood for any other that he can imagine—certainly not for the childhood of the boys of the upper classes who were sent away to public schools and never experienced the rich communal life of the streets. The street in which Henry lived as a young child is typical of the town of Castleford—one of the many small uniform red brick terraces, the houses having two rooms on the ground floor, two bedrooms above, and a coal cellar underneath the front room, which could be replenished with free coal from the pit through a trapdoor on the street. The terraces back on to each other and the intervening space is a lane on to which open the 'back yards'. At the end of the yards are the earth-closets and other outhouses, continuous with each other and making the lanes a walled space, wide enough to accommodate the horse-drawn 'soil carts' which emptied the closets every week. These lanes formed a maze-like labyrinth in which the children played whenever they were not at school.

The games they played were seasonal—ball-games in the winter, several different games with marbles, or 'taws', and above all 'piggy' or tip-cat—a game which was played with a stick (the bat) and a bail (the cat or piggy), a piece of wood about an inch thick and five inches long, sharpened at both ends. The game was played by tipping the cat at one end with the point of the stick and when it flew up into the air, hitting it as far as possible with the stick. The distance was then paced and compared with the achievements of other competitors. (I also played this game as a boy in Yorkshire and can recall the endless pleasure it gave.) All these games would be played until darkness fell, and if the children had strayed from their own pitch, they would then walk home through the misty gas-lit streets. Sometimes a gang from a rival school would be waiting in the shadows, and a fight between the two factions followed.

8 Castleford: the lane behind the Moore's house

Henry remembers the peculiar pleasure he experienced in making 'piggies' for the game of tip-cat, whittling the wood with his pocket-knife till it had exactly the right shape. Success partly depended on having a well-made piggy; it would only rise well if the angle at each end were perfect. This was perhaps Henry's earliest experience of a sculptural sensation. Another game involved modelling clay. I have already mentioned the fact that there were potteries in Castleford. The boys in Castleford could easily obtain clay from the neighbouring pits and with this they made little ovens, about four inches square, open on one side with a chimney on the top. At the right time of year, the late autumn, the boys went in search of touchwood (wood rotted to a powdery softness). When dry enough the touchwood could be lit by means of a piece of paper and then blown into a glow, the oven then making a magical object to carry round in the dark and keep the hands warm.

In summer the country was within easy reach and Henry and his friends would roam the lanes and footpaths, bird-nesting or gathering wild flowers. When Henry went to the Grammar School he made friends with the farmers' sons who came into Castleford for their education and at harvest time he often went out to the farms to help with the work. Living in such a small industrial town, on the border between town and country, Henry thus had the best of both worlds. It was not altogether idyllic—he remembers the cruelty of some of his companions when they suddenly found helpless living creatures like frogs in their power.

The home of the Moores at 30, Roundhill Road, still stands *(Pl. 9)*, just two windows and a door on each modest elevation, and the open yard at the back where the washing could hang to dry. Most of the daily life of the family was enacted in the one living-room (the 'back-room' with a kitchen range; the 'front-room' was kept for special occasions). Here the mother cooked and spread the table for the evening meal—the Yorkshire 'high-tea' which was ready for the father when he came home from the pit and had washed off the grime in a hip-bath placed before the kitchen fire. His wife scrubbed his back while the children played around. But the pits worked in three eight-hour shifts, so sometimes the father returned in the

9 Castleford: 30, Roundhill Road, where Henry Moore was born

early morning (4 a.m.) or late at night when the younger children had already gone to bed.

By the time Henry became conscious of his surroundings there would be five older children (not counting the one who died in infancy) and a younger sister, distributed over about eighteen years. When Henry was born his eldest sister Annie would have been fifteen or sixteen, capable of helping her mother with the upbringing of the younger children. Periods of unemployment meant extreme poverty for the family, and Henry remembers that a boiled egg was often halved between two children. But he never felt neglected or hungry: he was only conscious of loving kindness and security, and his childhood may be said to have been completely happy.

All the children were baptized into the Church of England, but the parents themselves were not ardent church-goers. The only occasion that Henry remembers his father going to church was for the funeral of his sister Elsie. Nevertheless (perhaps to give the children something to do on those long Sabbatarian days) they were sent to the Anglican church in the morning and to a Nonconformist Sunday-school in the afternoon. Henry's church-going fell off when he began to attend the Grammar School, but only because the homework in Scripture occupied the whole of Sunday.

At fifteen or sixteen Henry attended confirmation classes and developed a strong religious phase which lasted several months. 'I remember very clearly the day I was confirmed, feeling so good and so saintly as I went down the aisle that I didn't walk, I floated about four feet off the ground.'[2] But this religious phase then began to wane rather quickly, though he continued to attend church services spasmodically until he joined the Army.

The Sunday-school which Henry attended was the nearest to his home and belonged, as I have said, to the Nonconformists, not the Church of England. The superintendent of this school, after the prayers and hymns, would give a short talk or sermon, and more than one talk was to the effect that you must always listen carefully to what other people had to say, because no one person knew everything and there was a grain of truth to be picked up everywhere. On one such occasion the Superintendent told the story of Michelangelo, 'the greatest sculptor that ever lived'. He described how a sculptor's studio in those days would open on to the street, and how people passing by would stop to comment on the work in progress. On this particular occasion Michelangelo was carving the head of an old faun. A passer-by stopped and watched him for a while. The faun Michelangelo was carving was represented laughing, with all its teeth exposed. The man in the street eventually remarked: 'But you have given that faun all its teeth; an old faun would have lost some of them.' Whereupon the sculptor took his hammer and chisel and knocked out two of the teeth.

This was a decisive moment for Henry. He did not consider the moral of the tale—that an intelligent man is ready to take advice from any source. What remained in his mind was the image of Michelangelo, 'the greatest sculptor that ever lived', and from then onwards Henry became passionately interested in Michelangelo, and found out all that was possible about his life and work in the encyclopaedia that his father had bought him. An ideal had taken shape.

One other childhood sensation remained in the memory and was significant for the future. His mother suffered from rheumatism (probably rheumatoid-arthritis, for Henry remembers her swollen knuckles) and when Henry was old enough and strong enough she would ask him to rub her back with the strong-smelling liniment she herself made. The liniment smarted and brought tears to his eyes, but what was to endure all his life was the physical sensation conveyed by his fingers as they came in contact with the bones beneath the flesh. To the boy the expanse of the back—his mother was quite a large woman—seemed to be immense, and full of subtleties of yielding flesh and resisting bone that combined to give him a unique sensation which later he was to recognize as a specifically sculptural sensation, especially that sensation as elicited by the human body.

The family moved to a more commodious house at 56 Smawthorne Lane when Henry was about ten or eleven years old, but the environment did not change—the same red brick terrace houses, the same back lanes. But the country was a little nearer here; there were hawthorne hedges a few hundred yards away, in which Henry and his friends searched for moth chrysalids (to keep and hatch out in an empty match-box) and even found birds' nests. The silhouette of the pit-shaft was on the horizon and the slag-heaps were gradually invading the green fields, but the freedom of open spaces was always near, and the children had no sense of urban oppression. A poet like D. H. Lawrence grew up in exactly the same environment, and has described it for all time in books like *The White Peacock* and *Sons and Lovers*, and in some of his essays (e.g. 'Nottingham and the Mining Countryside'). Lawrence's Eastwood was essentially the same environment as Moore's Castleford, but Moore was never to experience the resentment and humiliation that Lawrence felt.

10 Castleford, another view

Lawrence projects an unhappy family life into his environment; his surroundings are ugly because his life is ugly. Moore had a happy family and he can say with Traherne: 'Some things are little on the outside, and rough and common, but I remember the time when the dust and stones of the streets were as precious as gold to my infant eyes, and now they are more precious to the eye of reason.'

CHAPTER TWO

Early Education

Henry Moore's education may be divided into three stages: elementary, secondary and professional. But these words indicate formal categories that tell us nothing about the actual process, which had little to do with categories and curricula, but was rather the direct influence of the places and people with whom the boy and then the youth came into accidental contact. A sculptor, like a poet, is born, not made; and I have already given a few indications of the presence, in Henry Moore, of an innate plastic sensibility which education might foster but could not create.

Henry went first to an infant school at the age of three or four, but at the age of eight he was transferred to the Temple Street elementary school, a co-educational or mixed school from which, at the age of eleven, he won a scholarship which gave him entry to the secondary school, now the Castleford Grammar School. He began his studies at this school in the autumn of 1909. He was lucky in that the school had an unorthodox headmaster called Thomas R. Dawes (affectionately known as 'Toddy') who had some feeling for the arts.

11 Caricature of T. R. Dawes by Henry Moore. Castleford Grammar School, c. 1915

Among the extra-curricular activities organized by this remarkable man were organ recitals of classical music, lectures by distinguished scholars, dramatic performances and a pageant of local history. Already at the elementary school Henry had been initiated into aesthetic experiences of this kind. There was a teacher there called John Holland who took the drawing lesson, and he soon discovered that Henry (like his brother Raymond before him) had a natural aptitude for design. He was entrusted with the designing of the school time-table, a calendar with a decorative border that was hung up in the classroom. Henry carried this artistic reputation to the Grammar School, but there he was to experience a set-back. Again he had been asked by one of the form-masters to do a decorative design for the classroom time-table, and Henry had drawn two

12 Temple Street Elementary School

figures to support a central panel. But the form-master was not the art teacher, who was a Miss Dowding. She came into the classroom and seeing Henry's design, began to criticize it. She pointed to the feet, which Henry had drawn hanging down in a frontal position, as they are often found in medieval manuscripts, and ridiculed them. Henry took a dislike to this art mistress, but the next year she was replaced by a Miss Alice Gostick, a woman of half-French origin who was the first to recognize the exceptional nature of her pupil's talents, and consistently encouraged their development throughout the decisive years of his education. She at once asked Henry to join in designing costumes for the school play, programme covers, and other such objects. There were two other boys who shared these activities with Henry—Arthur Dalby (who later became an Inspector of Art) and Albert Wainwright (who was much more sophisticated in his knowledge of art—he later became a theatrical scene-designer). The friendly rivalry that developed between these three schoolboys undoubtedly gave an early impetus to Henry's talents and ambitions.

Miss Gostick's influence was not confined to the school. She organized pottery classes for adults and persuaded Clokie's to allow the pots the children made to be fired in their kilns. She started weaving classes in which the parents of the children participated—all this at a time when art in the normal school consisted of patiently drawing and shading cubes and cylinders. She abolished the barrier between school and home, and would often invite her most promising pupils to tea on Sunday and show them the latest numbers of *The Studio*, a magazine that had an immense influence on the evolution of art at this period—it circulated throughout Europe and reproduced the work of the *avant garde* (*art nouveau* as it was called). There were other art books and magazines to feed the awakening sensibilities of these young artists, and always there was Miss Gostick's sympathy and enthusiasm. As an indication of the awakening of his plastic sensibility at this early age, Henry Moore once described to the author how he was able to recognize the girls in the school by the shape of their legs. 'If their bodies and features had been hidden by a board below which only their legs showed from the knees down, I could still have given a name to each pair.'

13 Castleford Grammar School. Henry Moore with Raymond Coxon and Arthur Dalby, c. 1920

When the time came for leaving the Grammar School, Miss Gostick interested the Chief Art Inspector of the West Riding in her three gifted pupils. A small number of art scholarships had been instituted which enabled the winners to proceed first to the regional colleges of art and from these, by a further process of selection, to the Royal College of Art in London. Before Henry had reached his final year at the Grammar School, under Miss Gostick's guidance his future career had been determined—to win these successive scholarships and become a professional artist. But first there was the parental prejudice to be overcome. Henry's father wanted him to follow the example of his eldest brother and become a teacher, to pass from the Grammar School to a training college, or even to the University of Leeds. But to become an artist—what kind of a career was that? 'You ought to do what your brother has done, get yourself qualified to earn a living, and after that, if you still want to become a sculptor, all right, but first get qualified.'

The First World War was to solve this dilemma, for Henry as for many other young men of that time, and since this too was an educational experience for those who were unexpectedly drawn into it, I shall include some account of it in this chapter. But Henry was only sixteen when war was declared, so for another two or three years he continued with his schooling. At the age of sixteen he passed the examination (the Cambridge Senior Certificate as it was then called) which gave him an entrance either to Leeds University or a teachers' training college. Henry then became a student teacher, and after one year's practical experience, he was for a few months a full-time teacher. He was then eighteen, and even teachers, if physically fit, could no longer be spared from military service. There was still a margin of choice between the various branches of the Forces, and on his father's advice Henry proceeded to London where certain special battalions of infantry and artillery were being formed, such as the Artists' Rifles, and the Civil Service Rifles. It was the first time that Henry had been in London, and the first time that he had had an opportunity to visit those treasure houses which were to play such an important part in his education, the British Museum and the National Gallery. He had found a room in an hotel in Southampton Row and presented himself to the two or three recruiting centres of his choice. He was accepted by the Civil Service Rifles, a battalion of the 15th London Regiment, and was drafted for training first to a camp on Wimbledon Common and then to one on Hazeley Downs near Winchester. From Winchester he could still visit London occasionally, but in the summer of 1917 he was sent to the Western Front in France. For three or four months he remained on a quiet sector near Arras, gaining the necessary initiation into trench warfare. Then late in that same year his Division was transferred to the Cambrai Sector, and Henry's battalion was detailed to hold positions behind Bourlon Wood taken earlier by the cavalry. Henry himself, in the course of his training, had joined a Lewis gunteam, and the team was sent forward to occupy an advance post. Here they were spotted by German planes and subjected to an intense bombardment. The advance post was a shell-hole in which they found a bottle of rum abandoned by some previous occupants. The lance-corporal

14 Henry Moore as a private in the 15th London Regiment (Civil Service Rifles), 1917

in charge of the team drank so much of this fiery liquid that he became incapable of directing the team, so Henry took charge. After three or four days of this intense fighting, during which the battalion made one advance over open ground, they were relieved. Out of a battalion of about four hundred, only fifty-two answered the role-call on arrival at the reserve position.

During the four days' bombardment a number of gas shells had been mixed with the ordinary shells, and though the effects were not immediate, about thirty of the fifty-two survivors began to show symptoms of poisoning. Henry was among them. He reported his sickness and was sent on foot to the clearing station, about ten miles behind the line. Meanwhile the poison had worked into his system and he became a stretcher case. He was sent back to England and then to a hospital in Cardiff, where he remained two months. After a further period in a convalescent camp he was moved to Aldershot for a course of physical training, and there he qualified as an instructor in physical training. As such he reported back to his regimental depot in Wimbledon and he remained there for the rest of the war as a specialist in bayonet drill.

His battalion was disbanded in the late summer of 1918 and Henry volunteered to return to France. He arrived there just as the Armistice was being signed, and remained in reserve, relieving his boredom by learning a little French.

As a teacher he belonged to one of the first groups to be demobilized. He left the Army in February 1919, but immediately applied for an Army grant (which was given to ex-service men to help them to rehabilitate themselves to civilian life). He resumed his teaching in Castleford from March to August, but in September entered the Leeds College of Art to continue his education.

War had been a brief adventure for Henry Moore. He did not experience trench warfare long enough to suffer the attrition of nerves and spirit that was the fate of less lucky men. He felt—and this is true of many who had a longer experience of war—that it had immensely widened his experience of human nature, and he had had time, in the long hours of waiting and watching which is an essential part of trench warfare, to consider what he would do if he survived. He was confirmed in his determination to become a sculptor. Once peace came nothing would hold him back from that ambition. The schoolboy who had been fired by the story of 'the greatest sculptor that ever lived' was now a man, his spirit disciplined by arduous dangers, his self-confidence established by the command of other men, his vision unshaken by the traumatic experience of war.

15 Moore as a student in London, c. 1926. (The carving was later destroyed)

CHAPTER THREE

Education through Art

Henry Moore began his studies at the Leeds College of Art in September, 1919. He travelled from his home in Castleford every day, catching a train in the early morning and arriving back about 10.30 p.m. During his first year at Leeds he prepared for the Drawing Examination of the Board of Education. He had expressed a desire to study sculpture, but there was no master to teach the subject. One was appointed in his second year, Reginald Cotterill by name, but Henry was his only student and not unnaturally they, master and pupil, grew rather tired of each other. Henry took to modelling on his own initiative. Leeds as a city was no more inspiring than the town of Castleford, and its Art Gallery contained little to Henry's taste except an exhibition of drawings and watercolours by the official 'war artists', Paul Nash, C. W. Nevinson and Wyndham Lewis. He also saw exhibitions of sculpture which included examples of the work of Rodin and Mestrovič. More important was the fact that there was still living in Leeds a man who had a profound influence upon all who came into contact with him—Sir Michael Sadler, the Vice-Chancellor of the University. Sadler had a collection of paintings and sculpture which was quite exceptional for its time—it included not only Constable, Turner, and other English masters, but also African negro sculpture[1] and works by Gauguin, Cézanne, Rouault, Matisse, Segonzac, Friesz, Chirico and Kandinsky. It was Sir Michael's son who, at his instigation, made the first translation of Kandinsky's *Ueber das Geistige* (*The Art of Spiritual Harmony*, London, 1914), and this book was read and discussed by art students in Leeds. Sir Michael used to invite the students of the College of Art to visit his house and see his collection, and this was Henry Moore's first contact with original examples of modern art.

At the end of his second year at Leeds Henry passed the Sculpture Examination and won a 'Royal exhibition scholarship' with which he could proceed to the Royal College of Art in London. It entitled him to a grant of £90 a year. Among his contemporaries at Leeds were Raymond Coxon, the painter, and Barbara Hepworth, the sculptor, who was born at Wakefield, only a few miles from Castleford. She was granted a scholarship by the West Riding County Council and accompanied Henry to the Royal College.

Henry spent the years 1921–24 at the Royal College. He took his diploma after two years and spent a third year in advanced studies, at the end of which he was awarded a travelling scholarship. His professor of sculpture was Derwent Wood, who was so overwhelmed by commissions for war memorials that he did little teaching, leaving such duties to an assistant, Will Coxon. More important, from Henry's point of view, was an assistant named Barry Hart whose duty it was to instruct him in the technique of stone-carving, pointing, etc. With Hart, and without the approval of his professors, Henry was allowed in his second year to experiment in direct carving.

At this time the director of the Royal College was a man of great distinction and wide culture, Sir William Rothenstein. Rothenstein was an artist himself, particularly interested in portraiture. He decided, as an experiment, to try modelling a head in clay, and for this purpose used the same studio as Henry. Thus began a friendship that was to have some important consequences for Henry. Rothenstein, though himself limited to an academic approach to art, was acquainted personally with many of the leading Impressionist and Post-Impressionist artists in Paris, where he had lived as a student and young man, and was quick to perceive that the student he worked beside was an artist of creative originality.

A decisive moment came when Henry, in the course of the curriculum, painted a composition entitled *Night*. It had been suggested to him by an Etruscan tomb in the British Museum, the lid of which is decorated with the reclining figures of a man and his wife (subsequently pronounced a forgery). The professor of architecture, Beresford Pyte, criticized Henry's composition in violent terms, and was heard to say that 'this man has been feeding on garbage'. Henry was very discouraged by this experience, and even thought of leaving the College; but Rothenstein spontaneously supported him and reassured him.

During all this time Henry was educating himself at the museums in London, and by reading. Two books had a decisive influence on him at this time—Roger Fry's *Vision and Design* (published in 1920) and Ezra Pound's *Gaudier-Brzeska* (published in 1916 but not read by Henry until he picked up a second-hand copy in 1922 or 1923). The most significant essay in Fry's book, which Henry had first read in the Leeds Public Reference Library, was a short one on 'Negro Sculpture'. Henry had already been attracted to this kind of sculpture in the British Museum, but here was a learned critic, and one with authority in the traditional spheres of art, who could attribute to craftsmen whose work had hitherto been regarded as of strictly archaeological interest 'the logical comprehension of form' and 'an exquisite taste in the handling of material'. Even more boldly Fry declared that 'some of these things are great sculpture—greater, I think, than anything we produced even in the Middle Ages... They have complete plastic freedom; that is to say, these African artists really conceive form in three dimensions.'

No less significant for Henry Moore was Fry's essay on 'Ancient American Art', in which perhaps for the first time in England a critic recognized the great beauty of Aztec and Maya sculpture.

In general, this book was an 'eye-opener' for the generation of artists in the 1920's, who learned that 'we may, then, dispense once for all with the idea of likeness to Nature, of correctness or incorrectness as a test, and consider only whether the emotional elements inherent in natural form are adequately discovered, unless, indeed, the emotional idea depends at any point upon likeness, or completeness of representation.'[2]

Vision and Design was a book that had a wide influence; *Gaudier-Brzeska*[3] was a book for specialists and particularly a book for sculptors. Henry Moore never met Gaudier-Brzeska, who was killed in action at Neuville St Vaast at the age of twenty-three. Henri Gaudier had been born in France (at St Jean de Braye, Loiret) on 4 October 1891 and at the age of fourteen had won a scholarship which took him to London. Another scholarship enabled him to go to Bristol and in 1911 he settled in London, living with a Polish woman, Sophie Brzeska, whose surname he added to his own. Gaudier was an artist of brilliant promise, and his achievement, even in the very few years that were granted to him, was impressive enough not only to give him a place in the history of modern art, but also to exercise a decisive influence on several artists in England, Henry Moore among them.

When Henry read Pound's book on Gaudier for the first time he found, among other significant statements, the following definitions from a manifesto which Gaudier first published in Wyndham Lewis' *Blast* in June, 1914:

> Sculptural energy is the mountain.
> Sculptural feeling is the appreciation of masses in relation.
> Sculptural ability is the defining of these masses by planes.

Each of these definitions gave expression to the ideals that were slowly formulating in the mind of the student at the Royal College of Art. A further passage, from an article written for *The Egoist* in the same year (a review of an exhibition organized by the Allied Artists' Association) was even more pertinent:

'The sculpture I admire is the work of master craftsmen. Every inch of the surface is won at the point of the chisel—every stroke of the hammer is a physical and mental effort. Not mere arbitrary translations of a design in any material. They (artists like Epstein, Brancusi and myself) are fully aware of the different qualities and possibilities of woods, stones, and metals. Epstein, whom I consider the foremost in the small number of good sculptors in Europe, lays particular stress on this. Brancusi's greatest pride is his consciousness of being an accomplished workman.'[4]

A further passage, from an article by Ezra Pound on Gaudier-Brzeska reprinted from the *New Age* and italicized by Pound in his book, anticipates one of Moore's own most significant statements (c.f. page 65):

'We have again arrived at an age when men can consider a statue as a statue. The hard stone is not the live coney. Its beauty cannot be the same beauty.'

Such was the 'garbage' upon which Henry Moore had been feeding while he was a student at the Royal College, but the great influences were not the words of these critics, but the works of art to which they referred. I shall mention later specific works of Gaudier, Epstein and Brancusi which may have influenced Moore, but for the moment it is sufficient to indicate the kind of intellectual ferment in which Henry Moore found himself during his years at the Royal College.

Derwent Wood resigned his professorship in 1924. Sir William Rothenstein asked Henry to take temporary charge of the school of sculpture while he looked round for a new professor. It is a sign of the esteem which Henry had already earned that Sir William freely consulted him about the possible candidates. Henry suggested Epstein, but Rothenstein wanted someone less masterful. He also objected to Henry's next suggestion, which was Eric Gill, and even to Frank Dobson. After months of deliberation the choice finally fell on Ernest Cole, a safe compromise—he might be described as a product of the same effete Parisian tradition as Rothenstein himself.

Henry seized the opportunity to take up the travelling scholarship that had been awarded to him in 1924, and went to Italy for several months. On his return Rothenstein offered him a position as sculptor instructor in the Royal College. During his absence in Italy Cole had objected to the choice of Moore, but Rothenstein, who throughout showed his strong sympathy for Moore, insisted on his appointment.[5] Henry took up the post and there followed a period of endless arguments with his superior. Cole remained at loggerheads with Sir William Rothenstein and eventually resigned. He was succeeded by Gilbert Ledward, but his point of view was no less academic and at the end of two years he presented Rothenstein with an ultimatum—he would not continue to work with Moore. But Rothenstein still persisted in retaining Moore. Ledward was succeeded by Richard Garbe, a Royal Academician whose prejudices were even stronger than those of his predecessor.

Henry meanwhile had accumulated enough work to hold his first exhibition, which took place in the Warren Gallery in Maddox Street in 1928. The previous year he had contributed to a mixed show at

16 The Royal College, c. 1929. Barry Hart; Professor Garbe; a student; Henry Moore; Alan Durst

the St George's Gallery, but the Warren Gallery exhibition was his first 'one-man' show and created a sensation. It received some adverse criticism but nothing to equal the outcry raised against the next exhibition, held at the Leicester Galleries in 1931. The art critic of the *Morning Post*, Richard Gregg, described Henry's work as immoral, bolshevik, etc., and suggested that it was a scandal that such a man should be a teacher at the Royal College. Professor Garbe took the article in triumph to Sir William Rothenstein and demanded the dismissal of such a dangerous man. Even the old students' association of the Royal College of Art passed a resolution against the presence of such an evil influence in the teaching world.

Henry held on until the end of his period of appointment, which had been for seven years, expiring in 1932. Towards the end of this period he was approached by Harold Williamson, the principal of the Chelsea School of Art, who had decided to open a department for sculpture. He asked Henry to be its first head. He accepted and remained in this post until the first year of the Second World War.

The Chelsea School was then evacuated to Northampton and though Henry occasionally paid visits to it, his teaching days were at an end. One incidental commission of great significance was a direct result of the move of the Chelsea School to Northampton. The vicar of the Church of St Matthew, Northampton, approached Williamson for advice about the commissioning of a sculptor to make a statue for his church. Williamson recommended Moore, and the *Madonna and Child (Pl. 134)*, whose significance in the development of Moore's work I shall discuss later, was the result.

The teaching period had lasted about fifteen years (from 1924–39), but it should be realized that at no time was Henry Moore exclusively a teacher. He usually spent two days a week at the Royal College, and afterwards the same amount of time at Chelsea. The rest of the week, and the whole of the long vacations, could be devoted to his own

17 Henry and Irina Moore after their marriage, 27 July, 1929

18 The studio at 11a, Parkhill Road, c. 1933

work. He went abroad from time to time—frequently to Paris, to
Italy in 1926 and to Spain in 1936. In 1929 (July 27) he was married
to Irina Radetzky, a student of painting at the Royal College. Irina
was the daughter of an Austrian father, Anatol Radetzky, and a
Russian mother. The father had been killed in the First World War
and the mother had remarried. In the confusion of the war and the
revolution that followed she had lost sight of her daughter, who
meanwhile had been educated in the Crimea and later in Moscow,
where she trained in the *corps de ballet*. Here she was traced by her
mother and in 1919 was brought to Paris by a Polish courier. She
went to school in Paris for two years and then, in 1921, came to
England, where she was given a home by the father of her mother's
second husband, who was an Englishman. She lived at Little Marlow,
went to school in High Wycombe and in 1929 proceeded to the Royal

19 At Burcroft, Kingston, Canterbury, c. 1937

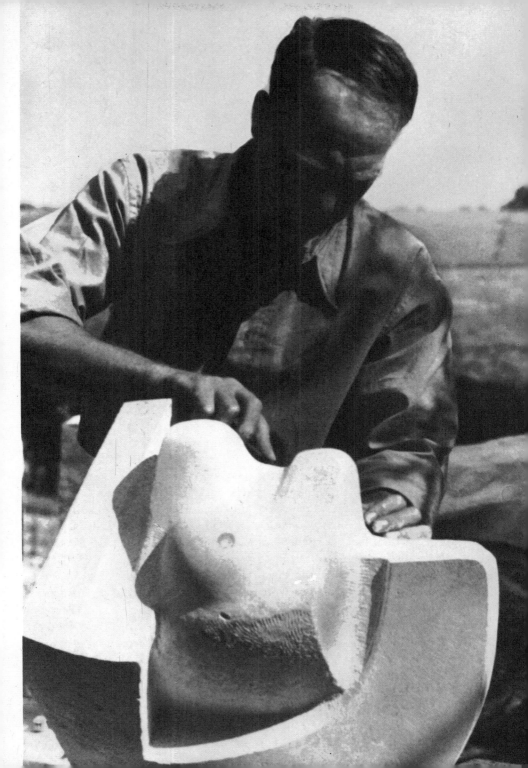

20 *Henry Moore with his daughter Mary*, c. 1950

College, where Henry first met her. They were married in the summer of this year and found a studio with living accommodation at 11a Parkhill Road, which is on the southern limits of the Borough of Hampstead. In 1931 they bought a cottage at Barfreston, a small village in Kent, where Henry could work during the vacations. Three years later they moved to another cottage at Kingston, near Canterbury, which had a large field attached to it and where Henry could fulfil his long-held ambition to work in the open landscape. They kept their London studio but it was damaged by bombs in 1940 so they decided to find a more permanent home in the country not too far from London. They found a small house in the village of Perry Green, near Much Hadham in the county of Hertford, and there they have continued to live ever since. A daughter was born to them in 1946.

21 Henry Moore in the maquette studio, Much Hadham

22 *Hoglands, Perry Green*

23 *(above right) The maquette studio, Much Hadham*
24 *(below right) The garden studio, Much Hadham*

Part Two

WORKS

CHAPTER FOUR

The Works: First Period 1921–25

The first phase of Henry Moore's development as a sculptor is one of assimilation and tentative experiment. It begins during his student years at the Royal College of Art but its products should not be regarded as the work of a student because, as we have seen, it was done in opposition to the teaching ideals of the College and largely outside the College, in the vacations.

The pieces that survive from this period are few but they clearly reveal the formative influences to which the artist submitted. Before describing these influences it is perhaps necessary to say something in general about the nature of this assimilative process in the development of an artist. One begins with the natural fact that man is an imitative animal. From birth he learns to cope with his environment, not merely by reacting to things, but also to persons, and particularly, of course, to his parents. If he is an artist he is born with a particularly acute sensibility; one of his senses is exceptionally keen, and sometimes developed at the expense of other organs of sensation. Such an exceptional child will inevitably be drawn towards those formal structures in his environment which give him most pleasure (or most displeasure) by their very existence, by their impingement on his senses. When in due course the child grows up and begins to find, among the objects in his environment, man-made works of art—that is to say, objects made with the intention of giving pleasure to the senses—then he will be attracted to them, they become the focus of his attention, and when he begins to make objects of his own he will inevitably imitate these models. Indeed, their very existence will stimulate him to make similar objects, but perhaps to make them more effective for his own sensibility, more nearly in accordance with his own sensuous reactions to experience.

This stage of imitation in an artist is as natural as the function of imitation in human development as a whole, but unless the young artist begins to experience some disparity between the significance of the model he imitates and the reality of his own feelings, he will remain what can literally be described as a second-rate artist, that is to say, an artist who lacks originality. He rises from this imitative second rank by a realization of the uniqueness of his personality, and a determination to find forms which, perhaps merely by minute variations of traditional forms, represent this uniqueness.

The artist's given nature will, of course, direct his attention in certain pre-determined directions. An absolute love of stone as a material, for example, will lead to a preference for certain kinds of landscape; a sympathetic relationship to human beings as such will lead to the attentive observation of their features and bodily shapes. Even a feeling for three-dimensionality, as opposed to flat surfaces, may be an innate rather than an acquired characteristic (always admitting that what we often call 'innate' may be a characteristic acquired in infancy rather than a physical heritage).

It is obvious that from the beginning of his apprenticeship to the art of sculpture, Henry Moore was attracted to certain subjects, to certain materials and certain techniques which 'suited his sensibility'. In the same way he was attracted to the work of certain contemporary sculptors, and to certain kinds of sculpture which he began to find in the British Museum. He freely and joyfully imitated these models, which were of three kinds:

1, historical, from the medieval gargoyles and other carvings which he copied while a student at Leeds in the nearby churches (Adel, Methley, etc) to the negro and Mexican sculpture he saw in the British Museum.

2, the work of contemporary sculptors: Jacob Epstein, Gaudier-Brzeska, Modigliani, Brancusi and Archipenko.

3, the work of sculptors and painters of the past, of whom the most important were Masaccio, Michelangelo and Rodin.

These are not chronological influences in Moore's career—for example, the medieval influence belongs to the Leeds period, whereas the Mexican influence did not begin before 1924 and is only fully

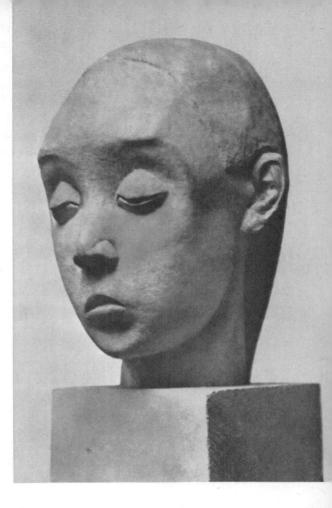

26 Head of a Girl, 1923

present in the reclining figure of 1929 *(Pl. 43)*. The influence of contemporary artists (a painter like Picasso must be included as well as the sculptors I have already mentioned) persists from the earliest surviving works of the Royal College period (the most important being the *Mother and Child* carved in Portland stone during the summer vacation of 1922, *Pl. 25*) to 1929, when it is superseded by the Mexican influence. Other contemporary influences may be assimilated after 1929 (I shall describe in the appropriate place the surrealist influence, which is mainly a question of Picasso). As for the third kind of model, this is much less direct. The assimilation of Mexican sculpture is formal and immediately obvious; the assimilation of the models provided by Michelangelo and Rodin should rather be called emulation. Their works are the supreme realization of certain sculptural principles which Moore had worked out for himself, in relation to tools and materials, and in the expression of certain humanistic ideals, and these great sculptors of the past are to be conceived as standards of comparison rather than as models to imitate.

Of the early contemporary influences acknowledged by Moore, the least obvious is that of Epstein. Epstein should perhaps be considered as a creative stimulus rather than as a model that was imitated. From the time he carved the statues to decorate the new building of the British Medical Association in the Strand, London, which was in 1908, he became and remained all his life a centre of controversy, and the philistine public in its ignorance conceived of him as the typical revolutionary artist, which he was far from being. No sooner had the controversy over the Strand statues died down than it was renewed by the tomb Epstein carved for Oscar Wilde's grave in the Père Lachaise Cemetery, Paris. The *Rock Drill* followed in 1913–14, a quasi-cubistic mechanistic figure, (more comparable to the work of a German expressionist like Rudolf Belling than to that of any of the Cubists) and was violently criticized in the Press. In 1920 a figure of *Christ* outraged the religious susceptibilities of the public, as did the monument to W. H. Hudson, *Rima*, which was defaced by hooligans as soon as it had been unveiled in Kensington Gardens. *Genesis* (1931) and *Adam* (1939) prolonged the controversy far into the career of an artist whose only ambition was to be placed in the tradition of the great Renaissance portrait-sculptors.

It is possible that two *Carvings in Flenite*, done about the same time as the *Rock Drill* and showing the influence of negro sculpture (of which Epstein became a discerning collector) may have had some direct influence on Henry Moore, but the odd fact is that the *Mother and Child* of 1922 seems to anticipate rather than imitate a figure like Epstein's *Genesis* (1931). The *Christ* of 1920, which at the time suggested to Father Bernard Vaughan 'some degraded Chaldean or

African, which wore the appearance of an Asiatic-American or Hun-Jew, which reminded me of some emaciated Hindu or badly grown Egyptian swathed in the cerements of the grave',[1] may have roused Moore to some sympathetic emulation in a work like the 1922 *Mother and Child*, though the formal influence in this figure is more precisely African than would be apparent from Father Vaughan's eclectic mish-mash of styles.

About thirty pieces between 1921–25 are listed in the Catalogue that appears in *Sculpture and Drawings I* but some of these have been destroyed. Of those that remain about half seem to show some influence of African negro sculpture, the other half the influence of

27 *Head of a Girl, 1922*

Gaudier-Brzeska, but these two influences are difficult to disentangle because Gaudier himself had been influenced by negro sculpture (the Easter Island sculptures in the British Museum may also be in question). The pieces by Gaudier[2] that are comparable are the marble *Torso* in the Victoria and Albert Museum *(Pl. 28)* which bears a strong resemblance to the clay *Torso* of late 1925 or early 1926 *(Pl. 29)*; the bronze *Fawn* and marble *Dog* which may be compared with Moore's *Dog* of 1922, *Horse* of 1923, and *Snake* of 1924 (LHI, 2, 7, 20); and *The Redstone Dancer (Pl. 30)* and *Boy with a Coney* which may be compared with the *Standing Woman* of 1923 *(Pl. 31)* and the *Caryatid* of 1924 (LH 1, 17). Gaudier's *Imp* of 1914 has a distinct resemblance to the *Caryatid* and his *Seated Figure* (also of 1914), to the *Standing Woman*.

28 Henri Gaudier-Brzeska. Torso, 1913
29 Torso, 1925–26

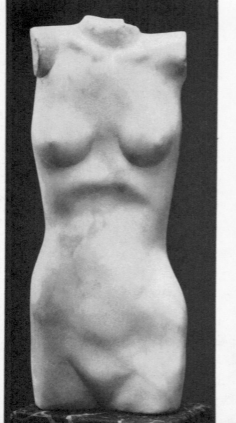
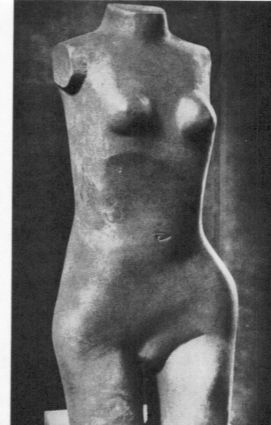

30 Henri Gaudier-Brzeska. The Red-stone Dancer, c. *1913*
31 Standing Woman, *1923*

33 Maternity, 1924

Discounting two or three pieces that show African influence (*Head of a Girl, 1922, Pl. 27*) and Mexican influence (two masks of 1923 and 1924, LH 1, 10, 21) there remain from this apprenticeship period a small and a large work which show the nascent power and originality of the young sculptor: the *Maternity (Pl. 33)* in Hopton-wood stone (1924) and the *Mother and Child (Pl. 32)* in Hornton stone of 1924–25 (now in the Manchester Gallery). The difference in scale (9 inches as against $22^1/_2$ inches) makes little difference to the monumental effect of these two pieces of direct carving. Here already the sculptor has perfect mastery of his

55

32 Mother and Child, 1924–25

medium. In the smaller figure the forms of the mother's half-length torso and of the child she holds in her arms are fused into one powerful rhythm, dominated by the grim concentrated face above them. In the larger figure, also half-length, the child is raised above the mother's head, its legs encircling her neck and held in position by the mother's arms, the right hand gripping the child's left leg, the left supporting its back. Again it is a rhythmical composition, but mounting like a pyramid, the base of which is the enlarged arm of the mother, the top the rounded skull and determined features of the child. Here for the first time we feel (rather than see) a 'haptic' emphasis on those elements in the anatomy which inwardly bear the greatest strain—a characteristic of primitive sculpture everywhere (and of children's art). Such exaggerations are determined by body sensations and not by visual experiences. Certain psychologists have demonstrated the existence of two creative types, a visual type which 'starts from his environment', whose 'concepts are developed into a perceptual whole through the fusion of partial visual experiences', and a haptic type who is 'primarily concerned with his own body sensations and with the tactual space around him'.[3] There is no doubt that from the beginning of his career haptic sensation has played a large part in Moore's representational forms.

By the end of 1925 Henry Moore had assimilated the main influences that were to determine the future course of his creative career. By 'assimilation' I mean a process whereby formal experience (i.e., the sensuous apprehension of three-dimensional form in all its manifestations) had been openly received and inwardly sifted. The process of 'testing' a formal experience is one that depends on the artist's initial sensuous endowment, and on the judgement of the relevance of any particular form to the feeling or intuition that the artist is impelled to express or re-present. At the beginning of 1926 Moore felt confident enough in his own powers of expression to go ahead and create his own world of form, but one image from the past was to remain dominant in his mind—the reclining figure of Chac Mool, the Mayan God of Rain (*Pl. 35*), which was to be the source of the most persistent and most significant symbolic form in the whole of his subsequent work.

34 Woman with upraised Arms, 1924–25

35 Chac Mool, the Rain Spirit, AD 948–1697

CHAPTER FIVE

The Works: Second Period 1926–30

Although by the end of 1925 Moore had absorbed the main influences that formed his style, it must not be assumed that the process of assimilation came to a sudden end. Apart from the Mexican influence which was to be dominant in the next five years, there were present in the background of Moore's subsequent development not only the general trend of the modern movement of which he had now become a member, but the individual practice of sculptors like Brancusi, Modigliani and Archipenko. I use the word *practice* rather than *style* because what the influence amounted to was not a direct imitation of formal characteristics, as had been the case with negro sculpture and the work of Epstein and Gaudier-Brzeska, but an emulation of the method of these other artists, particularly their devotion to direct carving. Modigliani's influence is to be seen perhaps only in one surviving piece—the beautiful *Head and Shoulders* belonging to Dr Henry Roland *(Pl. 37)*. This was carved in *verde di prato* marble in 1927, and though it is not strictly comparable to any one carving by Modigliani, the geometricization of the nose and lips may have been suggested by Modigliani's stone *Head* of 1913 *(Pl. 36)* which was presented to the Victoria and Albert Museum in 1922 and transferred to the Tate Gallery in 1952. The Royal College of Art at that time was part of the same complex of buildings in South Kensington. Students from the College were encouraged to study the sculpture in the Museum, and in this manner Moore became familiar with the Modigliani *Head*. Modigliani, however, could not have been responsible for the asymmetrical eyes in this piece; it is more likely that this particular distortion derives from Picasso's cubist portraits, though Laurens and Lipchitz display a similar feature in some of their early cubist sculptures (1917–19).

36 *Amedeo Modigliani.*
Head, c. *1913*

The influence of Alexander Archipenko is limited to one technical innovation, but an important one—the use of the hole as a device for relating the planes on the opposite sides of a piece of sculpture. It was already possible to effect such a relationship in classical sculpture by the articulation of the limbs of the human body, but the torso was left as an impenetrable mass. Classical sculptors, such as Michelangelo, had always been troubled by the tendency of these methods to limit the appreciation of a piece of sculpture to its frontal aspect. One of the chief aims of the modern sculptor has been to escape from this limitation and restore to sculpture its integral dimensionality, its 'all-roundness'. In Archipenko's *Boxing Match* of 1914 the masses are already rotating round a central hole, but a few years later, for example in the *Standing Figure* of 1920 in the Darmstadt Museum, the stone torso is deliberately pierced by a circular hole

37 Head and Shoulders, 1927

which is a substitute for a protruding breast *(Pl. 39)*. Archipenko's use of this device remained too deliberately geometrical; it degenerated into a decorative motive. Moore himself did not fully exploit the device before his Third Period (1931–36), but a suggestion of it is already present in, for example, the hollowed-out torso of the *Half-Figure* in cast concrete of 1929 *(Pl. 38)*.

The influence of Brancusi was almost of a moral kind. Moore visited Brancusi's studio in Paris—the first time anonymously, sometime before the Second World War, the second time in 1945 when he accompanied me to Paris to help to arrange an exhibition of contemporary British art sent over by the British Council. On this second visit Brancusi knew that he was entertaining a fellow-sculptor, for he had come to the opening of the exhibition. It was the first time he had emerged from the seclusion of his studio for many years, and in honour of the occasion he had dressed up in a long black coat and striped trousers. He admired Henry's work and the two sculptors were photographed together in front of one of the works on exhibition. When later Henry Moore revisited Brancusi's studio he was received with great warmth and there was a sympathetic exchange of impressions (one cannot say 'ideas' for there was some difficulty in communication due to language).

I have called Brancusi's influence a moral one because it was confined almost entirely to the preference they both shared for the technique of direct carving. Brancusi's significance for the whole development of modern sculpture proceeds from his devotion to the aesthetic qualities of the various materials he used—wood, stone, bronze—and his passionate belief that these inherent qualities could be revealed only by the artist's own hand, attacking the material with the appropriate tool and finding by slow sensuous manipulation the maximum aesthetic effect, in form and surface quality. This sometimes led (and this was Moore's considered reaction to Brancusi's work) to a precious quality (which the French call *chichi*); the surface quality becomes more important than the substantial mass. But in what some of his admirers would consider his greatest works, such as *The Prodigal Son*, 1914, in the Philadelphia Museum of Art or *Adam and Eve*, 1921, in the Solomon R. Guggenheim Museum, this

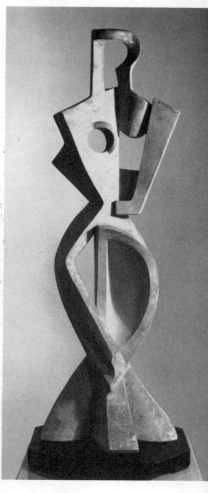

39 *Alexander Archipenko.*
Standing Figure, 1920

38 *Half-Figure, 1929*

criticism is not valid (Brancusi might have objected that since these two works are of wood, they demanded a different finish from works in marble or bronze).

I shall return to this question in considering some of Moore's later works, but for the moment I wish to emphasize the existence of a community of feeling between one of the first founders of the modern movement and a sculptor more than twenty years his junior. The significant influence of the master on the disciple, here as elsewhere in Moore's development, lies in a community of spirit animating both artists and not in a common language of form.

The contrary is true of the Mexican influence. The piece of sculpture most in question is a reclining figure of Chac Mool *(Pl. 35)*, a rain spirit of the Mayan culture (more precisely the Toltec-Maya culture whose centre was at Chichén Itzá in Yucatan, where the Mayas settled in the ninth century AD). On his visit to Paris in 1925 Moore visited the Trocadero Museum and there he saw a plaster-cast of the Chac Mool. The figure, carved out of limestone, reclines with head turned at a right-angle to the body and with knees drawn up. The

40 Reclining Woman, 1927

headdress consists of several strings of threaded beads which may represent grains of corn. Usually there is a breastplate in the form of a stylized butterfly and the figure is shown wearing bracelets, ankle-rings and sandals. The hands hold a flat receptacle on the stomach designed to hold sacrifices (said to be of human hearts).

Why did Moore become obsessed by this particular piece of sculpture? His own explanation is precise, but needs elaboration. In an article on 'Primitive Art' which he contributed to *The Listener* in 1941[1] he says that 'Mexican sculpture, as soon as I found it, seemed to me true and right, perhaps because I at once hit on similarities in it with some eleventh-century carvings I had been seen as a boy on Yorkshire churches. Its "stoniness", by which I mean its truth to material, its tremendous power without loss of sensitiveness, its astonishing variety and fertility of form-invention and its approach to a full three-dimensional conception of form, make it unsurpassed in my opinion by any other period of stone sculpture.'

The comparison with the stone sculptures on the Yorkshire churches must not be pressed too far, for these are small relief

41 *Reclining Woman, 1926*

sculptures and can only suggest some of the qualities of Mexican sculpture. It will be seen that with one possible exception these qualities, as analyzed by Moore, are all formal. They are: 1, truth to material; 2, power without loss of sensitiveness; 3, variety and fertility of form-invention; 4, full three-dimensionality of form. The exception to the purely formal nature of analysis is the suggestion of 'tremendous power', but it is clear that this also emanates from the form, otherwise Moore would not have immediately made the qualification 'without loss of sensitiveness'.

Erich Neumann, in his psychological analysis of Moore's work[2], attaches an arcane significance to the fact that in this statement,

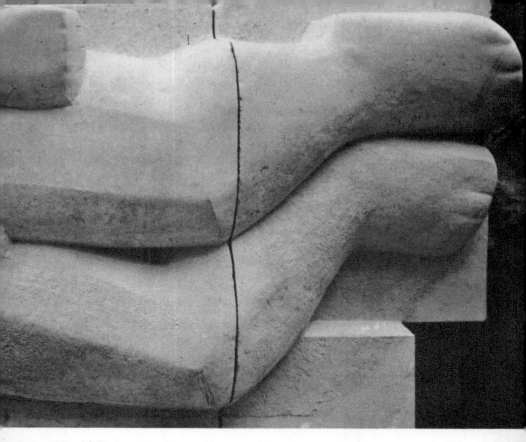

42 North Wind, 1928-29

which he also quotes from *The Listener*, Moore associates Mexican art with childhood memories—'an apparently psycho-analytical train of thought'. But in the psycho-analytical sense of the term Moore's recollection of the Saxon carvings at Methley and Adel are not 'childhood memories'; they date from his conscious student days and he was attracted to these carvings for the same reasons that later he was attracted to Mexican sculpture—purely formal reasons. This is begging the question of the psychological significance of form, but that question is a general one and not peculiar to Moore. Dr Neumann's conclusion, that Moore's intention in adopting (and adapting, for he changed a male form into a female form) this

43 (pp. 68-69) Reclining Figure, 1929

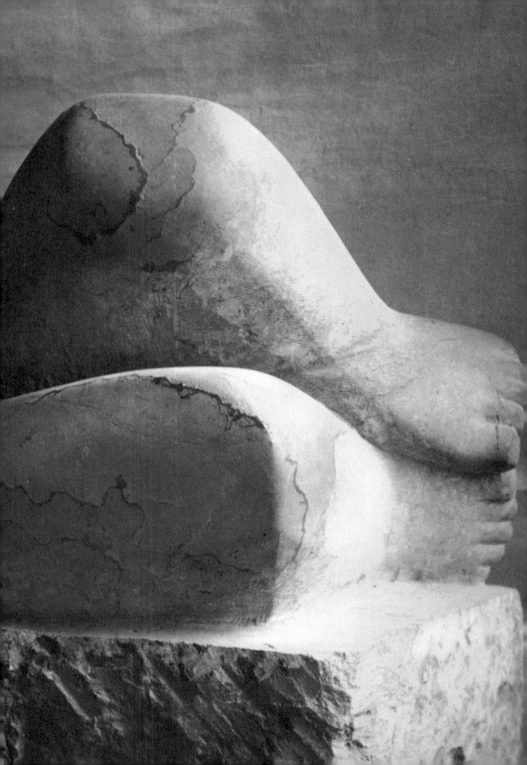

44 Reclining Figure, 1929

Mexican prototype into his own typical form was 'to create an archetypal and essentially sacral art in a secularized age whose canon of highest values contains no deity', is an elaboration that exceeds the aesthetic facts. Moore, in seizing on the particular form-invention represented by the Chac Mool, was primarily motivated by the fascination of the form, and cannot be said to have had as his 'true purpose', 'the incarnation of this deity in the world of today'.

Nevertheless, it must be admitted that Moore's obsession with this particular form-invention and his transformation of the figure from the male to the female has some arcane significance. But this significance is organic rather than transcendental, humanistic rather than deistic. What Moore incarnates in this first and all subsequent reclining figures is, first of all, a physical analogy or metaphorical comparison of the human (especially female) body and the earth eroded by natural forces into hills and hollows; and, beyond this, an aesthetic delight in the sensuous forms of the human body itself.

To identify Moore's reclining figures with the Great Mother or the Maternal Feminine, as Neumann does, is a psychological interpretation that may have some relevance to 'the irrational, subterranean laws of the creative process', but none to the immediate intention of the artist, which is always, in his own words, to make a piece of sculpture that is 'static' and 'strong', 'giving out something of the energy and power of great mountains'.

If we now note the differences between Moore's *Reclining Figure* of 1929 *(Pl. 43)*, in which the Mexican influence is first fully assimilated, and the Chac Mool itself *(Pl. 35)*, we shall see that they all tend away from the hieratic and spiritual significance of the prototype and more towards the earthy (tellurian) and humanistic (sensuous) qualities I have described. The features, though still stylized (nearer to Modigliani than the Mexican figure) are softened; one arm is lifted to support the head; softly moulded breasts rise from the torso and the legs are turned, partly to conform to the movement of the head, partly to assume

45 *Reclining Woman, 1930*

46 Reclining Figure, 1930

a more natural posture. The whole figure now moves with a rhythm which is far from the hieratic rigidity of the Chac Mool. One should note for comparison the *Reclining Woman (Pl. 40)* of two years earlier (1927), a small figure in cast concrete which has no obvious relationship to the Mexican figure and yet, in its general disposition of forms, anticipates the *Reclining Figure* of 1929. The similar figure of 1926 in bronze *(Pl. 41)* is even more relevant for comparison. All these comparisons suggest that the process of assimilation was gradual; it was four years before the 'shock of recognition' that had been experienced in the Trocadero found complete expression in the *Reclining Figure* of 1929.

The Mexican influence during this period also extends to a series of masks some in stone *(Pl. 49)*, some in cast concrete *(Pl. 48)*. But the five years we are surveying in this chapter were occupied mainly with the further development of the theme of the reclining figure, with a related theme which was Moore's first public commission (the figure of the North Wind which he carved in Portland stone for the Underground railway station at St James's Park in the autumn of 1928 and the spring of 1929, *Pl. 42*), and with several female busts, some of them representing a Mother and Child.

The *Reclining Figure* was carved between March and May. In the summer of this same year 1929, Moore was married and moved into a large studio at 11a Parkhill Road, Hampstead. Five reclining figures were carved here in the prodigious twelve months that followed; all show variations of the theme that remove it farther and farther away from its prototype.

The small alabaster *Reclining Figure (Pl. 44)* has the softened lines and compactness appropriate to such a delicate material. The *Reclining Woman* in Green Hornton stone *(Pl. 45)*, now in the National Gallery of Canada, is perhaps nearer in some details to the Mexican prototype (particularly in the mask-like face) but the breasts and raised knees are still farther away from the rigidity of the Chac Mool

47 *Reclining Figure, 1930*

48 Mask, 1929

49 Mask, 1929

and nearer to the mountainous, tellurian motive. A small reclining figure in Corsehill stone that has disappeared (LH I, 90) emphasizes this motive still more clearly by aligning the breasts and navel with the turned head and one raised knee. Finally, a small ironstone reclining figure (*Pl. 46*) shows a much stronger emphasis on an over-all rhythmical movement, also shown in the *Reclining Figure* in Ancaster stone of the same year 1930 *(Pl. 47)*. The stylistic debt to Chac Mool is still very evident, but the formal rhythm which runs without interruption from head to toes is Moore's own invention.

The figure of the North Wind perhaps deserves mention because it is the first evidence of Moore's success in marrying sculpture to architecture. The motive was prescribed (the three other winds were carved by other sculptors) and the figure had to be fitted into a cornice between the seventh and eighth floors of the building. This aided the conception because the elongated flying figure, with its upper arm streaming with a suggestion of wind-swept hair in alignment with the floating legs, makes an obvious but effective symbol.

50 Figure with clasped Hands, 1929

There remain from this very prolific period, not counting some miniature pieces and a few that were subsequently destroyed, sixteen or seventeen pieces of various sizes, the most important being the *Figure with clasped Hands* in Travertine marble, 1929, now in the Tel Aviv Museum *(Pl. 50)*, the *Half-Figure* in Ancaster stone, 1930, now in the National Gallery of Victoria *(Pl. 53)*, a *Seated Figure* in alabaster of 1930 *(Pl. 51)* and the *Girl with clasped Hands*, 1930,

51 Seated Figure, 1930

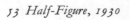
53 *Half-Figure, 1930*

52 *Girl with clasped Hands, 1930*

belonging to the British Council *(Pl. 52)*. The *Mother and Child* in *verde di prato* of 1929, *(Pl. 54)* belonging to Sir Kenneth Clark, deserves mention because in spite of its small size (4³/₄ inches high) it gives out a concentrated impression of monumentality. None of these pieces exceeds 30 inches in height, but they all have this same sense of contained power. The modelling is rhythmical, but at the same time conveys an hieratic dignity which suggests that the artist might have been looking at some of the Egyptian sculpture in the British Museum (note this quality especially in the Tel Aviv piece, *Pl. 50*).

54 Mother and Child, 1929

55 Mother and Child, 1929

Most of these pieces are in stone or cast concrete, but there are three figures in wood from this period, a *Torso* in African wood of 1927 *(Pl. 57)*, an ebony *Figure* of 1930 *(Pl. 58)*, and a boxwood *Figure* of the same year *(Pl. 56)*. All these wooden pieces are distinguished by a treatment which emphasizes the organic flow of the material and assimilates the bosses protruding from the figures (hair-knots, breasts, buttocks) to the nodular protrusions natural to wood. The result is a sculptural form that foreshadows the characteristic organic forms of the monumental reclining figures in wood of five years later.

56 *Figure, 1930*

57 *Torso, 1927*

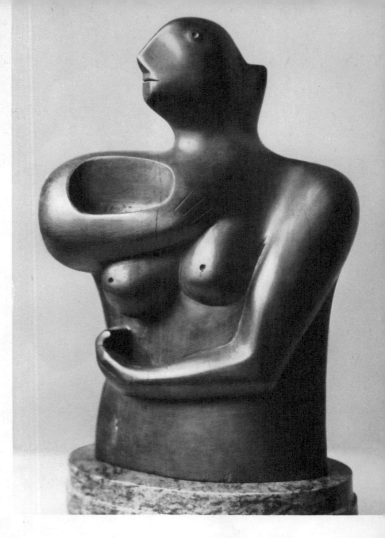

58 Figure, 1930

In general one may say of these five years, 1926–30, that they show the sculptor exploring materials and the forms appropriate to each material with ceaseless curiosity. Some of the experiments were to be rejected, but there remained a repertory of forms that could be exploited to their maximum effect in the great years that lay immediately ahead. Influences from other external sources might still arise and be absorbed, but the sculptor had now discovered his own plastic vision and had the means to realize it.

CHAPTER SIX

The Works: Third Period 1931–36

There is nothing in Henry Moore's external circumstances to explain the sudden leap into a super-realistic realm of forms represented by the Green Hornton stone *Composition* that he carved early in the year 1931 *(Pl. 59)*. It is true that in this year the sculptor bought a cottage at Barfreston in the county of Kent, where he worked during his vacations. This was also the period of crisis at the Royal College following the attack in the press on the work he had exhibited in the Leicester Galleries, which included the Green Hornton *Composition*. The period, from 1932 onwards, corresponds to his most intensive and enjoyable teaching period at the Chelsea School of Art. This is also the period when he lived in close association with artists like Paul Nash, Ben Nicholson and Barbara Hepworth who had studios in the same part of London[1]. But none of these events or experiences explains the proliferation of new forms in these five or six years. The forms in question did not displace the forms developed in the previous phase: the reclining figure, the mother and child motive, the general study from life (as we see from the drawings of the period) continued to develop uninterruptedly. The new forms are just as organic as the earlier forms (*all* Moore's work is organic, that is to say, derived from or analogous to the forms that result from natural processes of growth); but now the organism is violently distorted, to constitute the super-real forms of a new mythology of the unconscious.

Cycladic art of about 2,000 BC is the possible source of some of these distortions. Cycladic sculptures became known to Moore about this time, from their publication in Christian Zervos' *Cahiers d'Art* and elsewhere; one that he remembers in particular is the *Lyre-Playing Idol* in the National Museum, Athens *(Pl. 60)*. The whole

83

of this Cycladic material is relevant, for it made a strong impression on Moore at this time[2]. It may also have made some impression on Picasso a year or two earlier, though the comparison is not so exact in his case. In *Cahiers d'Art* for 1929 (vol. 4, pp. 342–54) Zervos published an illustrated article on 'Projets de Picasso pour un monument', and one of these projects in particular, a bronze of early 1928 *(Pl. 61)*, has some resemblance to Moore's *Composition* of 1931. Some of Picasso's paintings, sculptures and drawings of the years 1927–29 were also reproduced in a special number of *Documents* (Vol. II, No. 3, 1930), and Moore remembers acquiring a copy of this publication.

60 'Lyre Playing Idol', Cycladic Period

61 Pablo Picasso. Project for a Monument, 1928

Alfred Barr suggests other cross-currents that may have influenced Picasso and so indirectly Moore. 'It is probable that Picasso who was being courted by the surrealists at this time may have seen the early paintings of Tanguy; he surely knew the metaphoric figure paintings of his friend, Joan Miró. Possibly he felt the influence of the younger men but in any case these two series of sculptural drawings [Barr distinguishes the drawings made by Picasso at Cannes in the summer of 1927 and another series made at Dinard in 1928, both 'sculptures-que' in character] anticipate remarkably some of the biomorphic or organic abstractions and "human concretions" done by sculptors during the past fifteen years.'[3]

If there was a direct influence from Picasso's sculpturesque drawings, Moore made something very distinctive of it. Picasso's 'monuments' are far more arbitrary than Moore's compositions. Once having grasped the biomorphic image in all its surrealistic possibilities, Moore proceeded to develop its sculptural implications to a degree that Picasso never contemplated. Indeed, from now onwards, and right up to the present time, this surrealistic element constantly recurs in Moore's work. One might say that a tension was henceforth to exist which drew the sculptor in one direction towards more or less precise renderings of the human figure, and in the other direction towards three-dimensional 'metaphors', or 'biomorphs', that have no direct resemblance to natural forms, though remaining organic in feeling.

63 Reclining Figure, 1931

62 Relief, 1931

64 *Head and Ball, 1934*

65 *Bird and Egg, 1934*

This persistence of an organic element derived directly from the observation of natural forms forbids us to make any strict use of the term 'surrealist' in discussing Moore's work. It is true that Moore willingly participated in the International Surrealist Exhibition held at the New Burlington Galleries, London, in 1936, and his work has often been included in books and articles devoted to surrealism. His position in this respect is somewhat similar to Picasso's—a sympathetic participation in the movement but no commitment to explicit doctrine. Surrealism is by definition (André Breton's definition) 'pure psychic automatism, by which it is intended

66 Three-Piece Carving, 1935

67 Four-Piece Composition: Reclining Figure, 1934

to express, verbally, in writing or by other means, the real process
of thought. It is thought's dictation, all exercise of reason and every
aesthetic or moral preoccupation being absent.' It is true that in such
a definition Breton has the verbal rather than the plastic representation of the image in mind, but always in the work of surrealist
painters like Max Ernst and Salvador Dali, there is an attempt to
evade natural law, to dislocate perceptual images, to shock the
sensibility by illogical and unnatural collocations of images. This is
not the method of Henry Moore. Even in the most extreme distortions of the human body, such as those inflicted on the *Reclining
Figure* in lead of 1931 *(Pl. 63)*, there is an organic reference for each

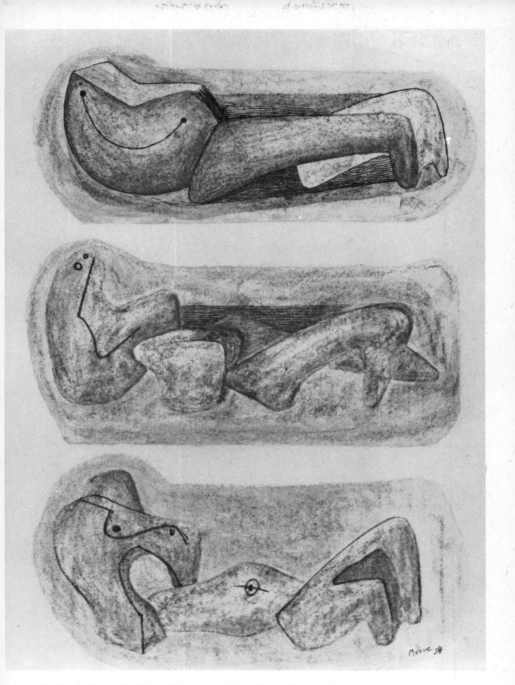

68 Study for a Reclining Figure as a Four-Piece Composition, 1934

69 Reclining Figure and Ideas for Sculpture, c. 1933

apparently arbitrary element—for example, in this particular figure the three rods that cross the hollowed chest refer to the ribs, and the thickening of the central rib is probably a vestigial breast. But this figure does not represent the extreme of this process of reduction. The plaster *Relief* of 1931 *(Pl. 62)* reduces the body to two nuclear extrusions in which, nevertheless, two eyes and a navel are to be identified. Three years later, in the *Three-Piece Carving (Pl. 66*; the original stone was destroyed, but Moore reproduced it in ebony the following year), and in the *Head and Ball* of Cumberland alabaster *(Pl. 64)*, the dislocation of the elements of the human body is carried to the degree of physical separation. Head, limbs and a round ball that might symbolize a breast lie like pebbles on a rectangular platform. A similar group in alabaster of this same year 1934, in the collection of Mr Harold Diamond, New York, is given the title *Bird and Egg (Pl. 65)* and conveys the alertness of such an animal.

70 *Composition, 1934*

71 Carving,
c. 1936

72 Square Form
1936

73 Abstract Drawing in colour, 1935

Other examples of this exploration of dislocated forms are the *Composition* in reinforced concrete of 1934 *(Pl. 70)* and the *Four-Piece Composition: Reclining Figure* in Cumberland alabaster of the same year *(Pl. 67)*. A glance at the drawings of these years (1933–34) shows more clearly how the separation of the corporeal elements was gradually achieved. The reclining figure in the pen and wash drawing reproduced in *Pl. 69*, itself already distorted into separate form-elements, is surrounded by more than twenty 'ideas for sculpture' which are in effect variations on the theme of the major figure. Some of these 'ideas' are minor variations of one idea, but the forms then proliferate in almost every conceivable direction until they reach (for example, on the left-hand side of this drawing) shapes which, if they were detached from the parent figure, could not be easily associated with the human form. Other drawings, e.g. *Pl. 68*

74 Square Form, 1936

show how the main elements of the human body, the head and shoulders, the belly and the legs, become separable masses each with its own formal identity.

This was not the end of the experiments in this prolific phase of Moore's development. If we look at the drawing of 1935 belonging to Lady Norton *(Pl. 73)*, we see the human body being subjected to a block-like 'cubization'. Instead of sinuous flowing forms, the body is made to conform to a rigid geometrical frame. In a drawing of the following year *(Pl. 76)*, the body begins to take on the appearance of an architectural monument, and in another drawing of the same year *(Pl. 78)*, such motives (the façades of two Greek temples) are actually placed in the background of a landscape setting for Moore's imaginary figures.

If we now turn to the sculptures of the year 1936 we find this same rectangular theme translated into stone. *Pls. 71* and *72* illustrate the extreme examples. The drawings tell us that these two forms, apparently so geometrical and abstract, are nevertheless derived from the human body. *Pl. 71* is called simply *Carving*, but the clue can be found in Lady Norton's drawing *(Pl. 73)*. *Pl. 72* is called *Square Form*, but its vitality comes partly from the intimations of a human body in the incised sockets and nipples. In fact, these two pieces, in spite of their near abstraction, have a far more powerful suggestion of animal vitality than some of the more representational sculptures, and another *Square Form* of this same year *(Pl. 74)* has the menacing aggressiveness of some primeval monster. Gentler in its suggestiveness, almost dove-like, is a carving in Brown Hornton stone of the same year *(Pl. 75)*.

75 Carving, 1936

*76 Two Stone
Forms, 1936*

Still recognizably a product of the same experiments in geometricization are two figures of a more monumental character, the
Two Forms in Horr.ton stone *(Pl. 77)* and the *Mother and Child* in the
same material *(Pl. 79)* both of 1936. One of the 'forms' in the first
piece has a window-like aperture such as we see in Sir Kenneth
Clark's drawing *(Pl. 76)*. The *Mother and Child*, which is 45 inches
high, dominates a landscape in its present location (outside Mr Roland
Penrose's house in Sussex) and is the forerunner of a whole series of
similar 'figures in a landscape'.

98

77 Two Forms, 1936

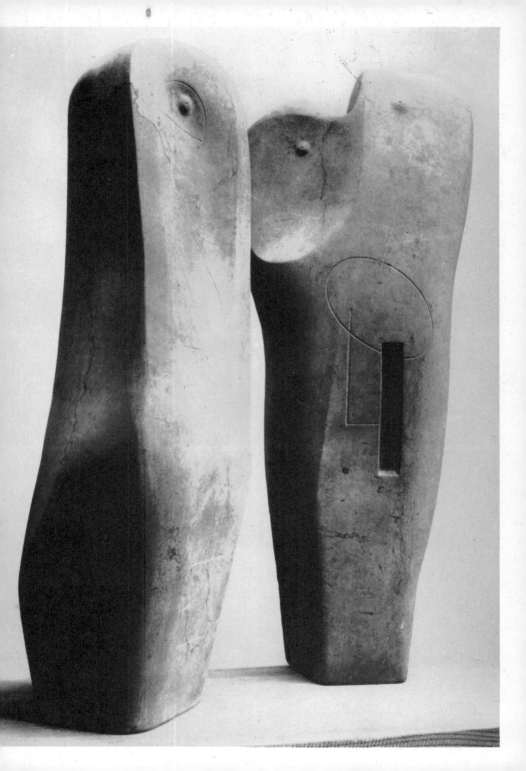

78 *Stones in
Landscape, 1936*

By isolating for consideration this series of 'biomorphic abstractions' I have misrepresented the complex development of Moore's sculpture during the six years now under consideration. The pieces so far described in this chapter take their place within a series of nearly eighty works which could be arranged in a sequence that runs from the near abstraction of the plaster *Relief*, 1931 *(Pl. 62)* or

79 *Mother and Child, 1936*

of the 1936 *Carving (Pl. 71)* to the near naturalism of the *Mother and Child* of 1931 *(Pl. 81)* or of the monumental *Reclining Figure* in carved reinforced concrete now in the City Art Museum of St Louis *(Pl. 80)*. An intermediate position in this sequence is occupied by some small carvings such as *Reclining Figure* in African wonderstone of 1934 (LHI, 141) and the *Carving* in the same material of the same year *(Pl. 82)*. The majority of the eighty works are, however, a logical development of a stylization of the human form already reached by 1930. The *Mother and Child* in *verde di prato* just mentioned follows in style and execution the *Mother and Child* in the same material of 1929 *(Pl. 54)*, the only difference being one which is increasingly evident in these naturalistic pieces—a softening of the rhythm. This

80 Reclining Figure, 1932

81 Mother and Child, 1931

serpentine gracefulness reaches its highest manifestation in the two wood figures illustrated in *Pls. 83* and *87*, where the graining of the wood is skilfully used to emphasize the contours of the forms. A supreme example of this flowing 'inscape' is the bust in African wood belonging to Sir Kenneth Clark *(Pl. 85)*. When, however, we turn to figures in stone, such as the *Mother and Child* in green Hornton stone of 1932 *(Pl. 84)* or the *Composition* in carved concrete of 1933 *(Pl. 86)*, or the *Figure* in Corsehill stone of 1933–34 *(Pl. 88)*, we

82 Carving, 1934

83 Girl, 1932

85 Composition, 1932

find the same dominant rhythm, as though the stone were intended
to imitate the structure of wood. But stone can also be grained,
and as we see clearly in the last-named piece, the geological stratifi-
cations are used for the same kind of formal emphasis. Any similarity
of form is due to the operation of the same physical forces in
different materials, and not to an arbitrary imposition of the form-
language of one material on the form-structure of another.

84 Mother and Child, 1932

86 Composition, 1933

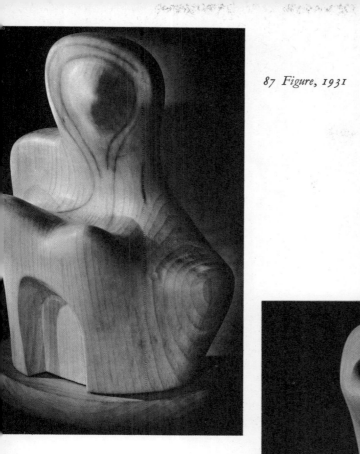

87 Figure, 1931

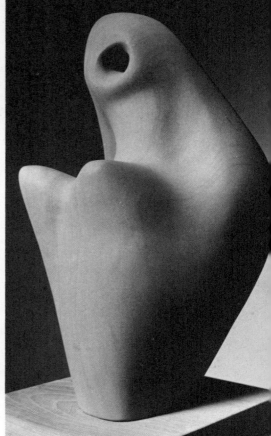

88 Figure, 1933–34

89 Composition, 1933

Sometimes the rhythmical principle seems to dominate the sculpture to the exclusion of any other structural elements. Two pieces will illustrate what I mean: the *Composition* in walnut-wood of 1933 *(Pl. 89)* and the *Two Forms* in ironstone of 1934 *(Pl. 90)*. It will be noted that in both these pieces the form is rounded off and is not given an artificial 'base'; it is an independent amulet, inviting the fondling hand rather than the stabile pedestal. The rhythm is, so to speak, freed from gravity; it has no end and no beginning. If we turn to the sculptor's drawings we can see how often the original conception is rounded off and floats in space: the foot or base is always a compromise in freely conceived sculpture.

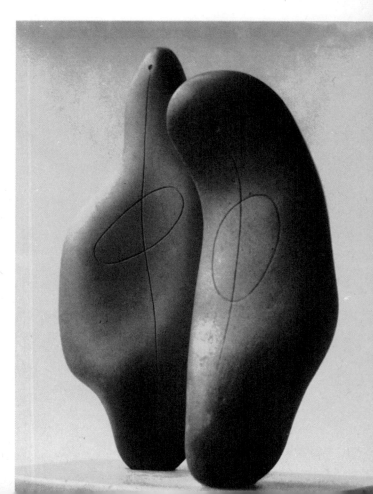

90 Two Forms, 1934

One more piece from this period deserves special mention: the *Two Forms* in Pynkado wood of 1934 belonging to the Museum of Modern Art, New York *(Pl. 91)*. It has, of course, a near relationship to the dislocated forms already considered, especially to the *Three-Piece Carving* of 1935 *(Pl. 66)*. But the piece that one may assume represents the head and breast curves over the smaller detached piece that represents the rest of the body (belly and legs). This is the first intimation of a motive—the protective uterine shell—that was developed into the lead *Helmet* of 1939–40 *(Pl. 105)* and finally given a monumental scale in the *Internal and External Forms* of 1951–54 *(Pls. 164–167)*. I shall say more about this motive when we come to these later pieces, but there can be no doubt that Moore, already in 1934, is groping (not a derogatory word in sculpture) towards what Neumann calls 'the conception of the body as a magical vessel, a transformative retort that is at the same time a mysterious cavern and a landscape', and this conception 'gradually brings about a strange transformation of the head, as though it too had been affected by the symbol of the body cavity. The head itself becomes the sheltering uterus'.[4]

The *Two Forms* of 1934 would hardly justify such an interpretation: the head is not yet detached and transformed into a cavity: the cavity is rather the breast over which the head leans protectively. The related pieces, and above all the contemporary drawings, make it clear that Moore arrived at this image, this plastic metaphor, by an analysis of the human form. We shall have to give serious consideration to the symbolic significance of the images evolved by the sculptor, but whatever assistance his sensibility may have received from the promptings of his unconscious, there is no doubt that forms have an evolution that is guided by laws of simplicity and economy, symmetry and rhythm, and that these laws in themselves are sufficient to bring about the creation of forms that are symbolically significant. The word 'significant' may beg the question, but it can be answered in physical rather than psychological terms. We must never forget the indissoluble union of form and matter. 'The Far Eastern masters, for whom space is essentially the theatre of metamorphosis and migration, and who have always considered matter as the crossroads where a vast number of highways come together, have preferred among all the substances of nature those which are, as it were, the most *intentional*, and which seem to have been elaborated only by some obscure art. On the other hand, these same masters, while working with the substances of art, often undertook to stamp the traits of nature upon them; they attempted, indeed, to transform them completely. And thus, by a singular reversal, nature for them is full of works of art, and art is full of natural curiosities.'[5] A work like Henry Moore's *Two Forms* is a natural curiosity, or originated as such; it is not conceptual in origin, but a perceptual image whose only origin is another image, that of the human body, which is a piece of nature 'full of works of art'. The most effective symbols (to adapt a saying of Picasso's) are those which we *find;* not those we seek.

91 Two Forms, 1934

CHAPTER SEVEN

The Works: Fourth Period

Sculpture 1936–40, Drawings 1939–45

The beginning of the next phase of Henry Moore's development can be associated with a definite event—his acquisition of the cottage at Kingston, near Canterbury, which has already been mentioned. Here for the first time he had a large field at his disposal. Moore took possession of the bungalow in 1934, but it was not until 1935 that he was able to acquire a load of Hopton-wood stone and work on a large scale against the open landscape. This had always been his ideal conception of sculpture—not a cabinet-art confined to small artificial spaces, but a monumental art standing freely on the ground, under the sky.

93 Reclining Figure, 1937

92 Sculpture, 1937

94 Head, 1937

This conception of sculpture is well illustrated in the photograph reproduced as *Pl. 92*, where the piece of sculpture, in itself only 20 inches long, is lifted on a big unhewn block of Hopton-wood stone and by virtue of its inherent monumentality can then dominate the landscape. The *Head* of the same year *(Pl. 94)* and the *Reclining Figure (Pl. 93)* have this same concentrated power, and are at the same time two of the most nearly abstract works ever carved by the sculptor. But each geometrical element in the composition, be it boss or hole, line or outline, remains subordinate to an organic complex, an icon imbued with natural animation. It is true that in this *Reclining Figure* the torso is reduced to a solid urn-like shape, but it remains an organic form, and the extensions (representing the limbs of the figure) flow from it with rhythmical ease.

There are two or three pieces of this year 1937 in other materials— Ancaster stone, Bird's eye marble (e.g., the compact *Figure*, *Pl. 95*), which belong to the same group of near-abstractions; and then, as a logical development from these compositions, there follows a series of stringed figures, one of the most original and fertile inventions of the artist.

95 Figure, 1937

In various pieces already discussed and illustrated, there can be found a linear convention, meant perhaps to represent ribs or fingers, but used merely as an accent on the otherwise rounded volume. A carving of 1934 now destroyed (LH I, 147) shows the first use of separate linear elements (in this case wires) to connect two protrusions from the surface of the stone. Then in 1937 and 1938 there comes a whole series in which string or wire is freely used, not merely as a device for relating two areas, but as dominant form elements. Such elements in a three-dimensional composition may have been suggested to Moore by certain mathematical models which he saw in the Science Museum, South Kensington, during his student days. The earliest and most extreme example of the type is the *Stringed Relief* in beechwood and string *(Pl. 96)*, a panel with protruding bosses laced together by about twenty taut strings. This piece may have been directly inspired by a mathematical model, but it also suggests a stringed musical instrument.

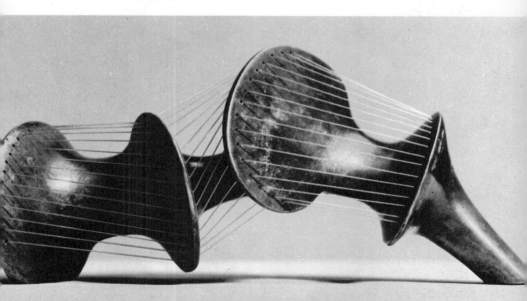

97 Stringed Figure, 1939

96 Stringed Relief, 1937

If one reviews the whole series of sixteen similar figures made between 1937 and 1940 *(see Pls. 96–101)* a biomorphic intention gradually emerges. There is one piece, a *Stringed Ball* of 1939 (LH 1, 198), which would seem to be strictly geometrical, but it is only 3½ inches high and may be regarded as a toy. Two stringed figures are called *Mother and Child (Pl. 101)*, another *(Pl. 100)* is called a *Bird Basket*; still another is called *The Bride (Pl. 98)*. All, however, with the possi-

98 *The Bride, 1939–40*

99 *Stringed Figure, 1938*

100 Bird Basket, 1939

ble exception of the *Stringed Relief* and the *Stringed Ball*, are bio-morphic in appearance and feeling, and they merge with other experimental compositions which are clearly related to the human figure.

David Sylvester, in the catalogue of the 1951 Tate Gallery Exhibition of Moore's work (p. 16), has suggested that 'the function of the string or wire is three-fold. It contrasts, in its tautness, with the curvilinear contours of the mass. It establishes a barrier between

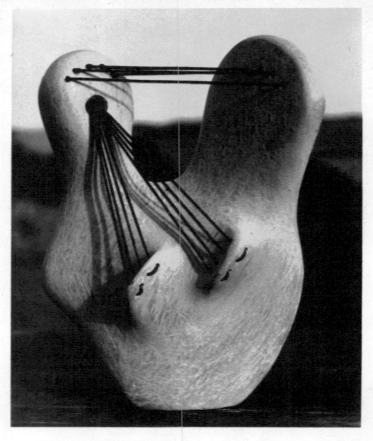

101 Mother and Child, 1938

the space enclosed by the sculpture's mass and the space which surrounds the sculpture—only, a barrier which, being a cage and not a wall, can contain the space on its open side while allowing it to remain visible. Above all, the string provokes movement of the spectator's eye along its length and thereby increases his awareness of the space within the sculpture—especially when, as in *The Bride*, one set of strings can be seen through another, so creating a counterpoint of movement which brings to life the space around and within which the strings operate.'

102 Reclining Figure, 1938

Related to this intermediate group is a series of lead figures, foreshadowed by the *Reclining Figure* of 1931 *(Pl. 63)* already discussed. Lead is a ductile material and true to his general principles Moore set about exploiting its characteristic qualities. In the *Reclining Figure* of 1938 *(Pl. 102)* (also reproduced in bronze) the molten flow of the metal is identified with the 'flow' of the body; breasts and knees and other protrusions hang downwards and coagulate like drops of lead poured from a crucible. In another *Reclining Figure* of the same year *(Pl. 103)* a modulated rhythm is imposed on the metal,

103 Reclining Figure, 1938

105 *The Helmet, 1939–40*

104 *Bronze Cast of*
Interior Figure for Pl. 105

which still, however, retains its pendulous tendency. The full exploitation of this ductile metal is reached in the *Reclining Figure* of 1939 *(Pl. 106)*, where the material outlines the volume rather than occupies it; here the body is reduced to an open structure which, however, is not a reduction of the flesh to reveal the skeletal substructure, but a merging of bone and flesh into one coherent rhythm.

An exceptional piece of this leaden epoch is the *Three Points (Pl. 108)*, which has also been reproduced in cast iron and bronze. This spicular object is a good illustration of the possibility of endowing an abstract form with an almost vicious animation. We know from a drawing of 1940 belonging to Mrs Moore *(Pointed Forms; Pl. 107)* that the points are evolved from the breasts of a female torso, but the geometricization of the motive has passed beyond any trace of humanity.

More significant of future developments is *The Helmet* of 1939–40 *(Pls. 104, 105)*, which consists of two separate pieces, an 'Interior Figure' (of which the artist possesses a separate bronze cast) and the helmet within which it stands. The helmet is womb-like and its frontal

106 Reclining Figure, 1939

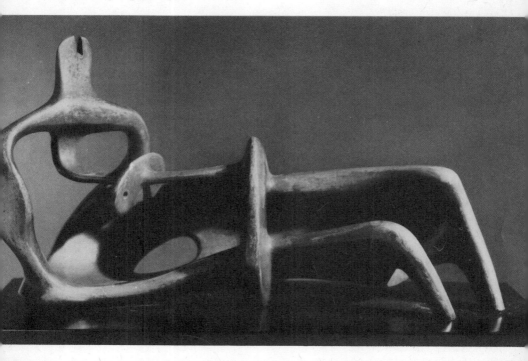

107 *Pointed Forms, 1940*
108 *Three Points, 1939–40*

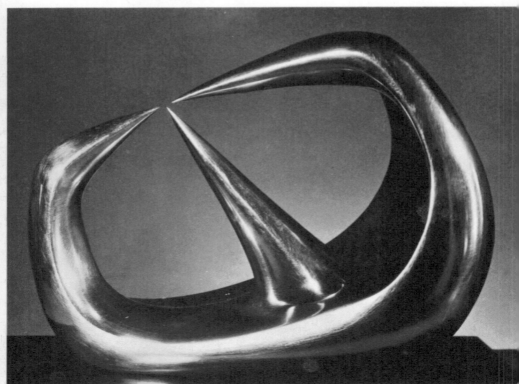

109 Figure, 1939

lobes move inwards to embrace and protect the enclosed figure, which is a rhythmical linear stylization of the human body related to the *Reclining Figure* of 1939 just discussed *(Pl.106)*. Helmet and figure are amalgamated into a single form in a lead *Figure* belonging to Mrs Patricia Strauss *(Pl. 109)*.

There remain from this pre-war period four major reclining figures, beginning with the elm wood *Reclining Figure* now in the Albright-Knox Art Gallery, Buffalo *(Pl. 111)*, which was begun in 1935 but not completed until 1936, proceeding to the elm wood *Reclining Figure* of 1936, now in the Wakefield City Art Gallery *(Pl. 112)*, and passing by way of the green Hornton stone *Recumbent Figure* of 1938 (July–September) now in the Tate Gallery *(Pls. 113–14)* to the elm wood *Reclining Figure* of 1939 (March–December) *(Pl. 115)*. They gradually increased in length, from 35 inches to 42 inches to 55 inches and finally 81 inches. As a series they achieve for the first time a monumental scale rivalling the masterpieces of the great sculptors of the past.

110 *Drawing, 1938*

111 Reclining Figure, 1935–36

Elm wood is a clearly striated material and Moore took full advantage of this fact to give visible contours to the volumes of his figures. The first of the series has a hollow torso, the open space uniting the back and front of the figure in one simultaneous rhythm. The upper limbs flow into the lower limbs without interruption; the head and breasts and shoulders are unified in one clasped knuckle-like tension. The ghost of Chac Mool is perhaps still present as a symbolic prototype, but the sculptor's own unique form-feeling now completely possesses the composition. The Wakefield figure is a larger version of the same composition, the lower limbs somewhat retracted, the whole form more compact. In translating the same composition into stone *(Pl. 113)* the figure becomes more naturalistic

112 (pp. 130–131) Reclining Figure, 1936

113–14 *Recumbent Figure, 1938*

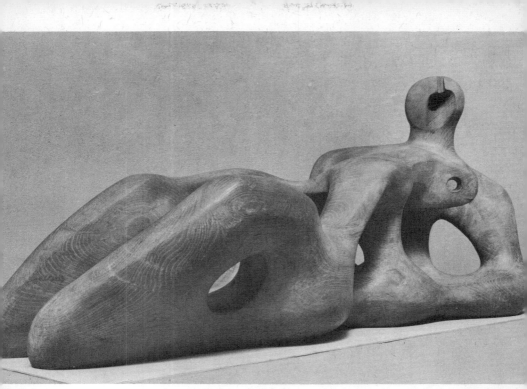

115 Reclining Figure, 1939

(especially the head and breasts), as though the harder material had put up more resistance to the eroding process of stylization. But when, in the later and larger *Reclining Figure* of 1939, the sculptor returns to elm wood, form regains its freedom. The human figure becomes a complex and hollow shell, a tense coil of shapes that define spaces as significant as their own sensuous substantiality. New conventions are found for the head and breast—annular protrusions that echo the body's hollow caves.

This figure marks a climax in Moore's development. Now came the interruption of the Second World War, and it was five years before he could conceive and complete his next major work, the Northampton *Madonna and Child (Pl. 134)*, which I shall discuss in the next chapter. The Chelsea School of Art was evacuated from London

116 Reclining and Seated Figures, 1931

in 1939 and Moore gave up teaching. He continued to live at Kingston as long as his material lasted—the last of the figures just discussed was carved there in 1939—but he returned to his London studio in 1940 and began to make drawings of the war-time scene, bombed buildings and people in the underground shelters. Since these are the most famous of all his drawings, I shall take this opportunity to discuss Henry Moore's drawings in general, and to estimate their significance in the evolution of his style.

134

117 Seated Figures, 1932

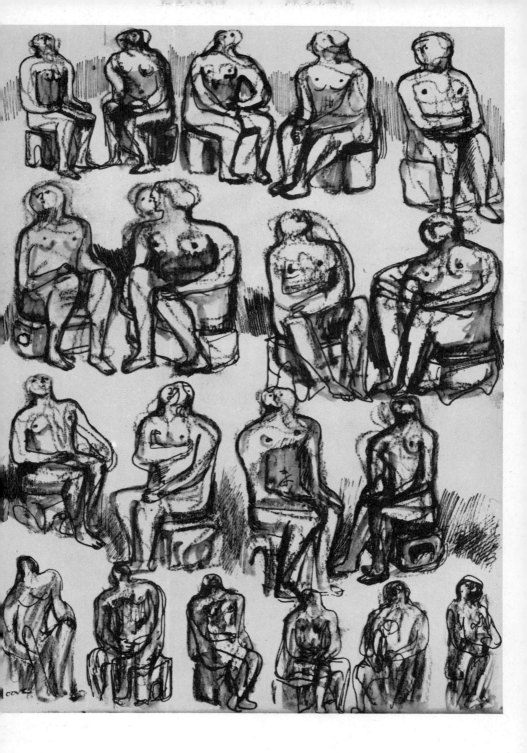

The Drawings

I have referred, and shall continue to refer, to specific drawings when they explain the genesis of a particular piece of sculpture, but there are two distinct types of drawings which recur throughout Moore's development. One type may be called working drawings—that is to say, drawings made 'as a means of generating ideas for sculpture'. To these should perhaps be added the life-drawings which Moore from his student days has made from time to time and continues to make. Quite distinct are those drawings, such as the Shelter Drawings, made as pictorial representations of observed scenes, and, by extension from these, drawings of imaginary scenes (such as the *Crowd looking at a tied-up Object, Pl. 119*). Naturally, whatever a sculptor may draw he tends to draw three-dimensionally, with a liberal use of chiaroscuro. His purpose, even if using only line, is to suggest space

118 Reclining Figure, 1942

119 Crowd looking at a tied-up Object, 1942

and the volumes occupying space. In 1937, before there was any question of making drawings with a documentary intention, Moore published an article in *The Listener* (18 August)[1] from which comes the phrase I have quoted above, but it must be quoted at greater length not only because it emphasizes the importance that this activity has always had for the sculptor, but also because it explains very clearly his working methods (and, indeed, the whole psychology of the creative process):

'My drawings are done mainly as a help towards making sculpture —as a means of generating ideas for sculpture, tapping oneself for the initial idea; and as a way of sorting out ideas and developing them.

'Also, sculpture compared with drawing is a slow means of expression, and I find drawing a useful outlet for ideas which there is not time enough to realize as sculpture. And I use drawing as a method of study and observation of natural forms (drawings from life, drawings of bones, shells, etc).

'And I sometimes draw just for its own enjoyment.

'Experience though has taught me that the difference there is between drawing and sculpture should not be forgotten. A sculptural idea which may be satisfactory as a drawing always needs some alteration when translated into sculpture.

'At one time whenever I made drawings for sculpture I tried to give them as much the illusion of real sculptures as I could—that is, I drew by the method of illusion, of light falling on a solid object. But I now find that carrying a drawing so far that it becomes a substitute for sculpture either weakens the desire to do the sculpture, or is likely to make the sculpture only a dead realization of the drawing.

'I now leave a wider latitude in the interpretation of the drawings I make for sculpture, and draw often in line and flat tones without the light and shade illusion of three dimensions; but this does not mean that the vision behind the drawing is only two-dimensional.

'...As far as my own experience is concerned, I sometimes begin a drawing with no preconceived problem to solve, with only the desire to use pencil on paper, and make lines, tones, and shapes with no conscious aim; but as my mind takes in what is so produced, a point arrives where some idea becomes conscious and crystallized, and then a control and ordering begin to take place.'

Up to 1928 Moore's drawings are straight-forward life-studies of the human figure in a natural pose, and as such are illusionistic: they are sculptor's drawings, comparable to the similar drawings made by Rodin, and convey a powerful suggestion of mass and volume. Then, with the studies of the reclining figure initiated by the Chac Mool, the natural pose is abandoned in favour of the formal variations that can be derived from the human body—significant distortions, as we have called them. It is only about 1931 that these distortions begin to exceed any illusionistic intention and to assert 'the sculptural idea'—that is to say, a shape that has 'associational, psychological

120 Figures in a Cave, 1936

factors' (Moore's own words) but which has left the original model
far behind *(Pl. 69)*. Then, about 1936, Moore begins to situate his
figures in a spatial environment. Interesting, as an anticipation of the
Shelter Drawings, is a drawing of this year representing *Figures in a
Cave (Pl. 120)*. In 1937–38 he made a whole series of 'drawings for
metal sculpture' *(Pls. 121, 122)* in which six or seven main figures stand
in front of a receding space occupied by the dim outlines of many
more similar figures. Then, year after year, ideas proliferate, shapes
pullulate, until sometimes a single sheet will contain as many as
thirty 'ideas', few of which were destined to be translated into solid
form. Many of these correspond to the period of the Surrealist
Exhibition and its aftermath (1936–39) and then they merge, almost
imperceptibly, into the first shelter drawings of 1940.

139

123 *Two Women, 1939*

121 *(above left) Drawing for Metal Sculpture, 1937*
122 *(below left) Drawing for Metal Sculpture, 1937*

124 Head of Sleeper. Page from Shelter Sketchbook, 1941

The Shelter Drawings were commissioned and had a precise intention—to depict the reaction of the people of London to the nightly bombardments inflicted on them by German aircraft. In their documentary function they are exact: they depict the groupings and poses of human beings confined to dim caverns far below the surface of the streets of London. Fear, expectancy, boredom, lassitude, mutual love and protection—all the emotions that were expressed in the attitudes of these victims of war are rendered in drawings of monumental power. The sculptor's eye is always present: to record the unexpected forms of limbs loosened by sleep, to register the subtleties of light and shade in the long dimly-lit 'tubes', to analyse the rhythmical groupings spontaneously assumed by people in a confined space. There is fantasy, too, as the light sometimes moulds the supine figures into unreal shapes.

125 Sleeping Positions. Page from Shelter Sketchbook, 1941

127 *Tube shelter perspective. Page from Shelter Sketchbook, 1941*

126 *Row of Sleepers, 1941*

128 Studies of Miners at Work, 1942

When this theme was exhausted I suggested to Moore that he might visit the coal-mines where his father had worked and find there forms of even more sculptural interest. The miners were engaged on war-work, so the subject came within the scope of his commission. He accepted the suggestion and went to the very colliery in Castleford where his father had worked. The result was a series of drawings that may not have the same emotional impact as the shelter drawings, but are of great power and dignity.

'Ideas for sculpture' were recorded throughout the war, and then in 1943 Moore was commissioned to carve a Madonna and Child for St Matthew's Church in Northampton, a significant work which I shall discuss in the next chapter. This commission turned his thoughts to the monumental group as such, and there followed a series of drawings on this new theme—the Family Group.

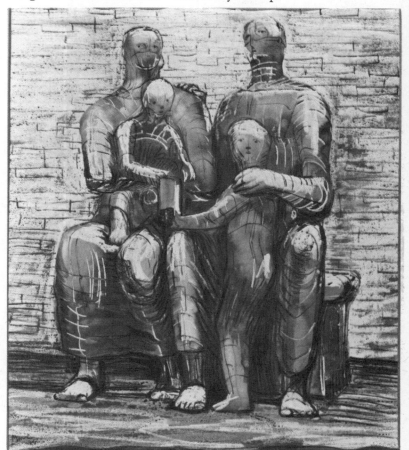

129 *The Family,*
1944

Family Group (Studies)   Moore

The birth of a daughter to the Moores in 1946 gave a further impetus to this humanistic interest, and for a short time encouragement seemed to be given to those people who had always hoped that the sculptor would abandon his extravagances and return to the academic fold. They were to be bitterly disappointed when, in 1950, he produced one of the most original concepts of his career, the *Standing Figures (Pls. 150–52)* for which preliminary drawings had already been made in 1948.

A word should perhaps be said about the technique of the drawings. Some (especially the earlier ones) are line and wash drawings, but later Moore made frequent use of waxed crayons, over the outlines of which the wash glides without being absorbed into the paper. He draws rapidly and instinctively, as if anxious to record the crowding images before they fade. Some drawings are more 'finished' than others; some are more directly related to the work in hand and others, as I have already said, are 'free'. But whether free or practical, they are all the drawings of a sculptor.

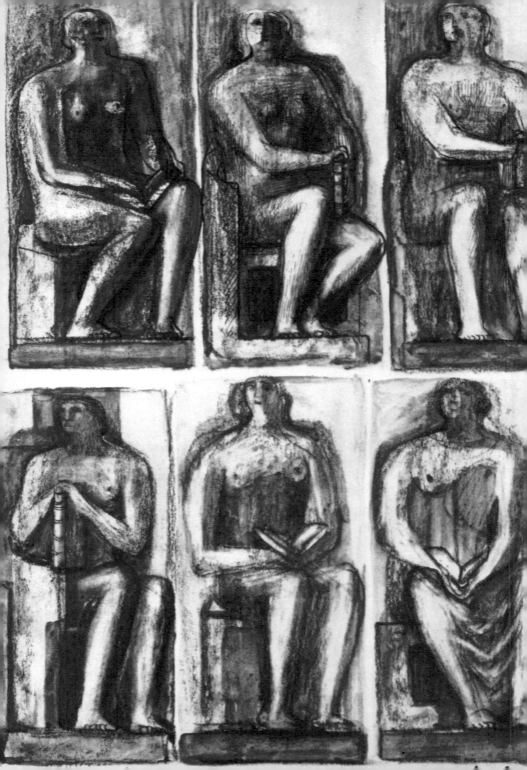

CHAPTER EIGHT

The Works: Fifth Period 1943–54

The final years of the war, 1943–45, were redeemed from frustration by three important commissions for public monuments. The first of these was the *Madonna and Child (Pl. 134)* which was commissioned by the Reverend Walter Hussey for the Church of St Matthew in Northampton (the donor was his father, Canon J. Rowden Hussey). The idea of a piece of sculpture to be placed in an architectural setting was not strange to Henry Moore—apart from the early relief of the *North Wind* done in 1928–29 for the underground building, St James's, London *(Pl. 42)*, Moore had been invited to carve reliefs for the exterior of the new Senate House of the University of London in 1938, but though he had prepared preliminary drawings, *(Pl. 131)*, Moore afterwards decided to abandon the project. These drawings show a 'Seated Figure' which already has the pose and monumental scale of the Northampton Madonna. The problem of the seating of the figure is already resolved, and even the holding, in two hands, of an object (a book instead of a child). The sketches and maquettes for the Northampton Madonna, though begun five years later, take up the motive exactly where it had been left in the drawings for the Senate House relief. There are differences to accommodate—a figure in the round rather than a relief, and the holding of a child instead of a book, but these are details that fit better into a sculptural conception. The relief as such had never appealed to an artist who has been pre-occupied above all with three-dimensional sculpture.

As a matter of fact it was decided from the beginning that the group should be placed against a wall of the Northampton church, so Moore did not have to contend with the problem that had caused Michelangelo so much trouble when he was commissioned for the first time to make a monument (his *David*) to occupy an exposed

131 Project for Relief Sculptures, 1938

position—a *space* rather than a *place*.[1] If a piece of sculpture has to be accommodated in an architectural niche, or be placed against a wall, what I have called 'a law of frontality' comes into operation— the sculptor has to convey the mass or volume of the figure without benefit of an all-round perambulation. It is a problem that had been successfully solved by the great sculptors of the Romanesque period, and superb examples exist, not only at French churches like Vézelay and Moissac, but also at Malmesbury Abbey in England. I might also mention, because it illustrates the same theme as Moore's Madonna, the defaced but still magnificent 'Virgin and Child' of the late eleventh-century in York Minster.

132 Madonna and Child,
1943–44. In progress

133 Madonna and Child, 1943–44. In progress

The Romanesque sculptors solved the problem by using the involuted folds of the garments to create a dynamic flow of lines which give the illusion not only of vitality but also of depth, and this is essentially Moore's solution in the Northampton Madonna. The folds of the Madonna's robe are greatly simplified in comparison with the Romanesque figures, to allow breast and knees to emerge as solid bosses, in harmony with the rounded heads of the Madonna and the Child, and also to achieve a feeling of serenity as against the more agitated movement of the Romanesque figures. But the same impression of integral form and monumental independence is also created, and the group takes its place within the architectural setting (a neo-Gothic church of considerable dignity) with perfect assurance.

The formal problem was not the only problem raised by this commission: there was the problem of the religious or symbolic content of the work. It is, of course, naive to assume that all religious works of art are products of a religious sensibility. Devout artists such as Fra Angelico are the exception rather than the rule. In executing commissions with a specifically religious theme, the artist must, of course, respect certain conventions: the symbolism is pre-ordained and in the Middle Ages the details of the execution were laid down with some precision. But the artist, in the degree of his skill, is a technician who welcomes a difficulty to be solved, and the representation of a religious symbol, even of a religious emotion, is a challenge to his skill. The emotion that is generated in the course of his work is aesthetic, but it runs in predetermined channels.

Henry Moore himself has discussed this problem in a written communication which was printed in a leaflet issued to celebrate the Jubilee Festival of the church of St Matthew in September, 1943:

'When I was first asked to carve a Madonna and Child for St Matthew's, although I was very interested I wasn't sure whether I could do it, or whether I even wanted to do it. One knows that religion has been the inspiration of most of Europe's greatest painting and sculpture, and that the Church in the past has encouraged and employed the greatest artists; but the great tradition of religious art seems to have got lost completely in the present day, and the general level of church art has fallen very low (as anyone can see from the affected and sentimental prettiness sold for church decoration in church art shops). Therefore I felt it was not a commission straight-away and light-heartedly to agree to undertake, and I could only promise to make notebook drawings from which I would do small clay models, and only then should I be able to say whether I could produce something which would be satisfactory as sculpture and also satisfy my idea of the 'Madonna and Child' theme as well.

154

'There are two particular motives or subjects which I have constantly used in my sculpture in the last twenty years; they are the 'Reclining Figure' idea and the 'Mother and Child' idea. (Perhaps of the two the 'Mother and Child' has been the most fundamental obsession.) I began thinking of the 'Madonna and Child' for St Matthew's considering in what ways a Madonna and Child differs from a carving of just a Mother and Child—that is, by considering how in my opinion religious art differs from secular art.

'It's not easy to describe in words what this difference is, except by saying in general terms that the 'Madonna and Child' should have an austerity and a nobility, and some touch of grandeur (even hieratic aloofness) which is missing in the everyday 'Mother and Child' idea. Of the sketches and models I have done, the one chosen has I think a quiet dignity and gentleness. I have tried to give a sense of complete easiness and repose, as though the Madonna could stay in that position for ever (as being in stone she will have to do).'

As I said in my Introduction to *Sculpture & Drawings* Vol. I, the qualities mentioned by Moore in this confession—austerity, grandeur, quiet dignity and gentleness, complete easiness and repose—even hieratic aloofness—are all qualities that can be immediately related to formal values. They are qualities that can be related to Buddhist art or Egyptian art, indeed, to great art of any kind, secular as well as religious. The only specifically religious element that can be embodied in a work of art (and this is not specifically a Christian element) is what is sometimes called *numinosity*, by which we mean mystical or transcendental values that are suggested but not defined— the beauty of holiness, to use a Biblical phrase. But (and again I have said this before) it is impossible to distinguish between the beauty of holiness and the holiness of beauty. Beauty, embodied in a work of art, is a transcendental value, as many mystics and theologians have been prepared to admit. 'Climb up upon this height and you will see how the paths of beauty and of holiness approach each other, growing distant, until finally in the far distance they can no longer be told apart.'[2]

For all its 'hieratic' qualities, the Northampton *Madonna and Child* remains human and accessible: the group symbolizes maternity, but the mother and her child are as 'natural' as the prototypes of similar religious themes represented by a Renaissance artist like Masaccio. The features, for example, are just sufficiently stylized (i.e., removed from the realism of a particular model) to make them universal. The austerity or aloofness proceeds from the monumental scale and from the broad simplicity of the style.

It was a natural transition from this work to the further commissions that followed in the course of the next five years. Immediately after the *Madonna and Child* came a series of Family Groups, beginning with the sketch-model in terracotta of 1944 *(Pl. 135)*, of which there are no less than seventeen, culminating in the large

135 Family Group, 1944

136 Family Group, 1945

scale (5 ft) group in bronze at the Barclay School, Stevenage, in the county of Hertfordshire *(Pl. 139)* (three other casts·were made, one of which is in the Tate Gallery, another in the Museum of Modern Art, New York, the third in the collection of Mr Nelson D. Rockefeller). The sketch-models are all within a height of 5 and 7 inches except two that immediately precede the final group (e.g., *Pl. 137)* which are 16 or 17 inches high. The addition of another adult figure, the father, and sometimes an additional child, immensely complicated the form problems, and one sees the sculptor trying various devices for unifying the group. Sometimes it is done by carrying the same piece of drapery over both pairs of legs *(Pl. 135)*, sometimes by joining together the arms of the mother and father, and once *(Pl. 137)* most daringly, by bringing the parents' knees together and unifying the two knee-borne children by the same sweep of drapery. Every

137 Family Group, 1947

138 Detail of Pl. 139

group provides a different solution and there is a considerable variation in the degree of stylization—from the near naturalism of the first sketch-model *(Pl. 135)* to the surrealist split-head of the father in the working-model of 1945 *(Pl. 136)*. In the Introduction to Volume II of *Sculpture & Drawings*, after commenting on the continuity of these family groups, I suggested that this surrealistic element in 1945 points forward to the most significant group in the next phase of Henry Moore's development, the *King and Queen* of 1952–53 *(Pl. 176)*, 'an advance into the superhuman realm of myth. This king and queen never reigned in our world—they were crowned in Erebus, or perhaps in some Olympian grove. They are figures of mystery or fate: they look calmly into futurity.' It is one more illustration of the complex interweaving of plastic motives in the development of Moore's sculpture.

139 Family Group, 1945 and 1949

141 Madonna and Child, 1943. Sketch–models

Two minor commissions may be mentioned here. The *Madonna and Child* commissioned in 1949 by Sir Joseph Ridley for St Peter's Church, Claydon, Suffolk *(Pl. 140)*, is based on one of the terracotta sketch-models shown in *Pl. 141* (the third from the left with the crown from the model second from the left) and is therefore closely related to the Northampton Madonna, though not so large in scale or so monumental in effect. Still smaller in scale (17 inches high) is the bronze *Seated Figure* commissioned by the British Film Academy (LH 11,3); instead of a child the female figure holds a sprig of laurel, but the figure itself is closely related to the maquettes for the Northampton Madonna.

The Family Group theme already mentioned as the first of the maquettes *(Pl. 135)* was originally commissioned by the late Henry Morris, Director of Education for Cambridgeshire and a discerning patron of the arts, for a Village College at Impington (an educational project dear to Morris), but it was never possible to raise the

163

140 Madonna and Child, 1943 and 1949

142 *Reclining Figure, 1945*

necessary funds. Almost ten years later (1954–55) a stone group based on the maquette was erected in Harlow New Town as the central feature of a new housing estate.

Before passing on to the major works of the next five years it should be noted that many of the maquettes we have just discussed were reproduced in bronze, usually in editions of seven or nine. Between 1943 and 1947 more than one hundred and forty bronzes were cast, and their diffusion to collectors and museums throughout the world helped to establish the fame of the sculptor. There were purists at the time, devotees as Henry Moore himself had been of the 'mystique' of direct carving, who deplored this development in his technique, and imputed it to a loss of integrity. There was some outward pressure due to the scarcity of carving materials during the latter part of the war, but Moore was already using a metal, lead, as early as 1929, and this material used freely in 1939–40 led naturally to the bronze Family Groups of 1944 onwards. Moore became fascinated by what he has called 'the bronze thing'—that is to say, the forms natural to a casting in this metal. The change of technique

143 *Reclining Figure, 1945*

involved a change of approach: it was no longer a question of the material (stone) imposing its qualities on the ideas of the sculptor: the ideas could now be rendered without physical compromise into a ductile material. The forced suspension of carving during the war had given the sculptor an opportunity to reconsider his ideals, and he began to recognize, not the error of his previous dogmatism, but its limitation *in terms of sculptural form*. In direct carving the appeal is partly a superficial one—the sensuous quality of the stone or the wood. But forms, or formal images, exist independently of a particular substance: ideal forms that should be rendered without any compromise due to the intractability of the material. To work in clay, wax or plaster allowed the formal idea to emerge without compromise, or with only those compromises due to physical laws of gravity and flow. Constructivist sculptors like Naum Gabo had always maintained that the sensuous appeal of the material was a seduction that interfered with the direct expression of three-dimensional form, and though Moore never accepted the abstract idealism of the Constructivists, he agreed on this point, and found

that henceforth he could use modelling and casting as an appropriate medium for the representation of the formal images that were crowding in upon his mind.

The supreme expression of this new freedom was to be the *Standing Figure* and the *Double Standing Figure* of 1950, but before we discuss these important pieces there are three other major pieces to note—the *Memorial Figure* in Hornton stone placed in the garden of Dartington Hall, Devon; the elm wood *Reclining Figure* now at Cranbrook Academy, Bloomfield Hills, Michigan; and the *Three Standing Figures* in Darley Dale stone erected in Battersea Park, London (the gift of the Contemporary Art Society). All are large-scale works. The Dartington figure *(Pl. 144)* is closely related in style

144 Memorial Figure, 1945–46

145 Three Standing Figures, 1947–48

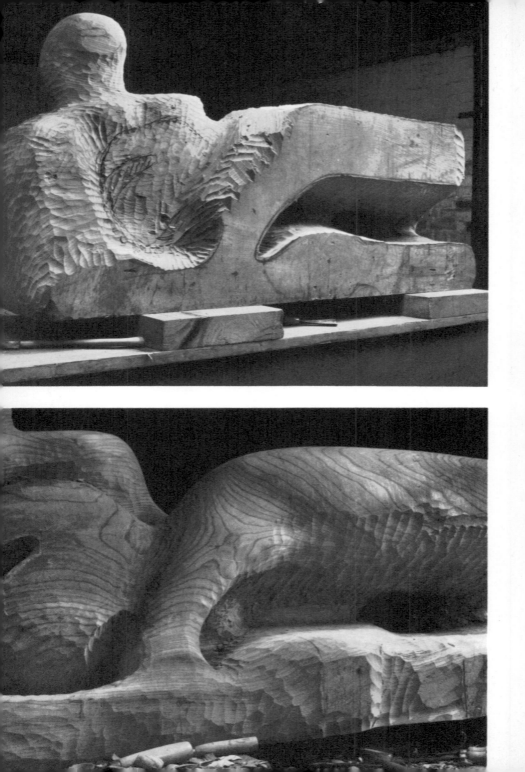

to the Northampton Madonna—it has the same rhythmic flow of draperies, the head has almost identical features, and from it emanates the same feeling of aloof calm. The *Three Standing Figures, (Pl. 145)* which was carved in 1947–48, that is, four years later than the Madonna, is the first monumental group done for an open public place—it was done specifically for an exhibition of sculpture in the open park and after the close of the exhibition was given a permanent setting on the sward against a background of trees. Again we have a strongly emphasized rhythmical treatment of the human figure, and a convincing solution of the problem of relating three upright figures to each other and to an overriding plastic unity. The stylization of the heads is carried a good deal farther than in the Madonna:

148 *Reclining Figure, 1945–46*

they become periscopic organs, total eyes that range the infinite space around them.

The elm wood *Reclining Figure (Pl. 148)* was carved between the autumn of 1945 and October, 1946. It is 75 inches long and one of the largest works executed by Moore to that date. Photographs showing its evolution from the block have been preserved *(Pls. 146–147)*. They show a rhythmical configuration being gradually imposed on the original reclining-figure motive, and a desire to open up the solid forms to allow the rhythmical movement to penetrate throughout the mass. The 'rings' of wood are skilfully used to emphasize the contours, and to carry the lower limbs freely along the body's extent.

A *Reclining Figure* in brown Hornton stone *(Pl. 149)* (now in the possession Mr Henry R. Hope, Bloomington, Indiana), and two *Reclining Figures* in bronze *(Pls. 142 and 143)* may be considered as preliminary studies for the Cranbrook figure. They carry the configuration of the material to an extreme rhythmical emphasis, and, to reach this extreme, open out the torso into flowing ribbons of metal or stone—the figure of 1945 *(Pl. 143)* has an elegance that might be called rococo, anticipated in the lead *Reclining Figure (Pl. 102)* of seven years earlier.

None of these major or minor pieces of the years 1945–48 prepares us for the radical innovation of the *Standing Figures* of 1950 *(Pls. 150–152)*. There is a drawing of 1948 *(Pl. 151)* which indicates more explicitly the origins of the separate formal elements—shoulder-blades are triangulated (or identified with a triangular torso) and the arms are made continuous with the legs. What happens in the final sculptural realization of the image is a splitting of the human frame along the lines of force indicated by arms and legs with a nodular joint at the shoulders, hips and knees. The shoulder-blades are extruded as triangular wedges, while the neck is again split to end in two antennae-like heads.

The two figures can be viewed independently or in association; they are essentially outdoor sculptures, and look best in a landscape setting, as on the open fells of Mr Keswick's estate at Shawhead, Dumfries, Scotland. From a formal point of view there are anticipations of the figures among the five interiors for the lead *Helmet*

Head of the same year *(Pl. 160)*, and as far back as the drawing of 1933 *(Pl. 69)* all the structural distortions are clearly indicated. There are similar indications in the *Drawings for Metal Sculpture* of 1937 *(Pls. 121, 122)*. It is essentially a concept for metal, for a tensile open structure, but the sculptor has endowed the form with overtones of watchfulness, of expectancy, of menace. Moore once told me that the preliminary idea had come from a photograph he had seen of some tall African tribesmen who stand perfectly still in the marshes of a river delta intent on spearing fishes.

The sculptor's output in the years following the conclusion of the war was so prolific that it is only possible to select for mention those

149 Reclining Figure, 1946–47

pieces that show a significant formal innovation. The series of *Rocking Chairs*, for example *(Pls. 154 and 155)*, is an ingenious extension of the Mother and Child motive, and was no doubt inspired by the young daughter that had been born to the Moores in 1946. There are many drawings of this period that reflect domestic scenes, for example, the charming *Family Group* of 1951 *(Pl. 153)* (this drawing also illustrates the 'contouring' that Moore often introduces into his drawings, in this case interlocking outlines that give the drawing a jig-saw puzzle effect). The rocking-chair motive is repeated in 1952, and the following year the Mother and Child motive assumes a more sinister aspect in a bronze in which the child is seen aggressively attacking the mother's breast with its gaping,

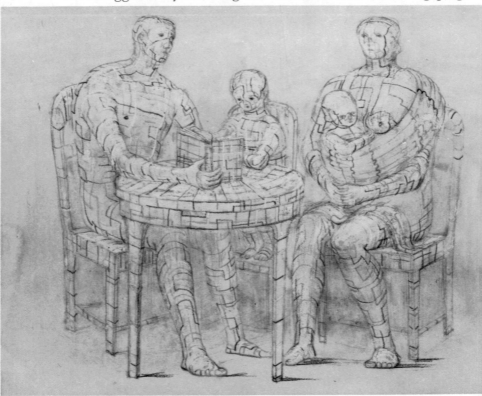

153 Family Group, 1951

154 *Rocking Chair No 3, 1950*

155 *Rocking Chair No 2, 1950*

*156 Mother and Child,
1953*

bird-like beak while the mother's terror is expressed in a sharply
serrated head *(Pl. 156)*. This group is so close an illustration of the
psycho-analytical theories of Melanie Klein that it might seem the
sculptor had some first-hand acquaintance with them; but the artist
assures me that this is not so. It may be that, in Neumann's words,
'it is a picture of the Terrible Mother, of the primal relationship
fixed forever in its negative aspect'[3], but if so, it is a picture that
comes from the artist's unconscious: it has no direct connections
with any psycho-analytical theory.

Small reclining figures were made from time to time, usually maquettes for larger figures. The helmet motive is resumed in 1950 (Pls. 158, 160), this time with a series of five alternative 'interiors'. The helmet is the same protective shield as before, though more elaborate; the interiors are biomorphic fantasies, four of them with eyes on the end of antennae like extensions which, when inserted in the helmet, stare from the open visor, giving the object an intense vitality. Two years later (1952) the helmet motive is resumed, this time joined to the shoulders (Pl. 159).

157 Three Standing Figures, 1953

158 *Helmet Head No 2, 1950*

159 *Helmet Head
and Shoulders, 1952*

160 *Five Figures (interiors for lead helmets), 1950*

161 (left) Leaf Figures Nos 1 and 2, 1952

162 Relief No 1, 1952

In 1952 another series of minor pieces begins with the bronze *Leaf Figures (Pl. 161)*. In these figures the shape and surface of the female body are assimilated to the outlines and veining of dead leaves, with a mainly decorative effect, but the motive is extended in the same year to the *Reclining Figure* illustrated in *Pl. 163* in which the skirt of the figure takes on a leaf-like sweep that adds one more variation to this persistent motive. Another variation of an earlier

163 Reclining Figure No 5, 1952

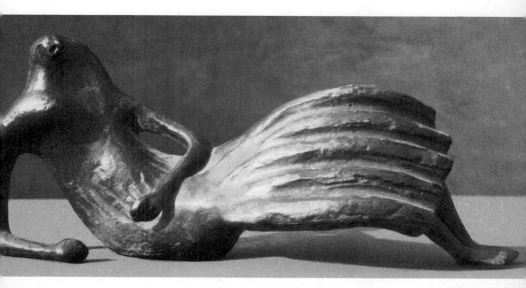

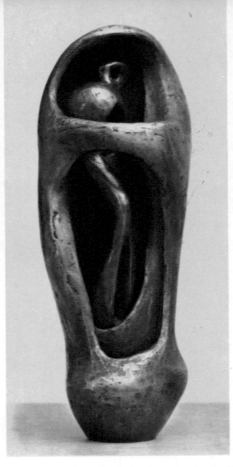

164 *Maquette for Upright Internal and External Forms, 1951*

motive is the gigantic (103 inches) *Internal and External Forms* of 1953–54. A bronze maquette for this piece was cast in 1951 *(Pl. 164)*. This was followed in the same year by a working model in bronze *(Pl. 165)*, 24½ inches high, of which seven copies were made (examples in the Rhode Island School of Design, USA; Art Gallery, Toronto, and Kunstmuseum, Basle). A large-scale plaster model was then made (1952–53) and, finally, the still larger version, which is carved in elm wood *(Pl. 166)*.

This is one of the sculptor's major works and unique in that the carved form was preceded by a careful exploration of the formal possibilities in modelled clay or plaster. The forms appropriate to wood were visualized from the beginning, but it cannot be said

165 *Working Model for Upright Internal and External Forms, 1951*

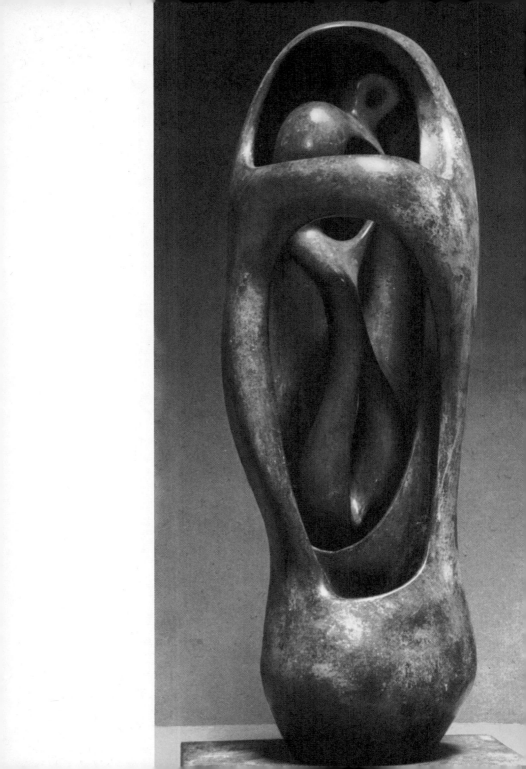

167 Detail of Pl. 166

that the material determined the forms, which are rather the archetypal forms of womb and foetus. It is tempting to quote Neumann
once again, because from his point of view this piece is the culmi-
nation of Moore's creative symbolism:

'It is no accident that this figure reminds us of those Egyptian
sarcophagi in the form of mummies, showing the mother goddess
as the sheltering womb that holds and contains the dead man like
a child again, as at the beginning. Mother of life, mother of death,
and all-embracing body-self, the archetypal mother of man's germinal

166 Upright Internal and External Forms, 1953–54

ego-consciousness; this truly great sculpture of Moore's is all these in one. And just for that reason it is a genuine bodying-forth of the unitary reality that exists before and beyond the division into inside and outside, a profound and final realization of the title it bears: *Internal and External Forms*. Outside and inside, mother and child, body and soul, world and man—all have been made "real" in a shape at once tangible and highly symbolic.'[4]

This supreme achievement is an upright form. Not content with this solution of the problem Moore decided to make a horizontal

168 Working Model for Reclining Figure (Internal and External Forms), 1951

169 Reclining Figure (External Form), 1953–54

or 'reclining' version. First there is again a working model in bronze
(Pl. 168) and then a final version which is 84 inches long *(Pl. 169)*.
The open forms in this reclining version are more complex and the
internal form is more introverted and secretive. The over-all form is
more organic and shell-like, and though the analogy of the human
body is clearly intended, it is a natural formation of universal
significance, recalling the sculptor's early obsession for caves and
eroded rocks. 'Woman', as Neumann says, 'has become the vessel
absolute, the place of entrance and exit, a pure earth form made of
cavities and hollows.'

170 *Animal Head, 1951*

171 *Goat's Head, 1952*

172 Mother and Child Nos 1 and 2, 1952

Equally chthonic or earth-bound are the *Animal Head* and *Goat's Head (Pls. 170, 171)* of the same time (they come between the working model and the final stage of the reclining *Internal and External Forms)* and these lead to the rough projects for sculpture on the corner of a building *(Pl. 172)*. Moore is feeling towards the *King and Queen* of 1952–53, and several minor figures that exploit the same formal idea, for example a *Seated Woman on a Bench*, 1953 *(Pl. 173)*, and two *Seated Figures* of 1952 and 1952–53 (LH II, 76 and *Pl. 174*). The maquette for the *King and Queen* follows (LH II, 79) and finally the full-scale bronze, 64½ inches high.

189

175 (right) Head of King,
1952–53

173 Seated Woman on a Bench, 1953

174 Seated Figure, 1952–53 (detail)

176 King and Queen, 1952–53

This major work, like the *Standing Figure* of 1950, is best seen on the kind of site for which it was intended, such as the fells at Shaw-head *(Pls. 176, 177)*. From a formal point of view the figures repeat the conventions worked out for the family groups of 1944–45, though as befits their royal dignity, there is no attempt to link the two figures together. They are influenced by the leaf-forms of the same year—the torsos are shield-like and hollowed at the back, the robes hang perpendicularly from the knees. The two heads give the group its air of mystery. They have evolved from the heads of the immediately preceding standing figures and leaf figures, but they have acquired a superhuman power that seems to have come straight from

177 Another view of Pl. 176

Greek mythology—and it is significant that in the previous year, 1951, Moore visited Athens, Mycenae and Delphi. The nearest equivalent to the fantastic shape of these heads (and to the spatulate form of the torsos) is found in the clay figurines of the thirteenth to fifteenth century BC found at Mycenae, but the scale is not comparable, and the King's head in particular has a more obvious connection with the animals' heads of the same year (compare *Pl. 175* with *Goat's Head, Pl. 171*). The magical effect of this group may be said to spring from a combination of regal dignity and animal vitality, but this complex conceived in relation to a *genius loci*, a place haunted by tragedy like Mycenae or Delphi.

178 Warrior with Shield, 1953–54

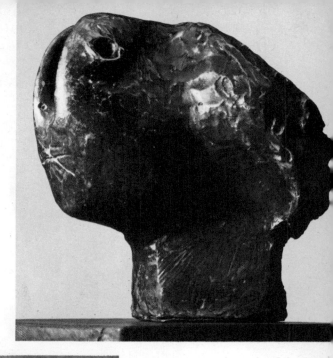

179 Warrior's Head, 1953

*180 Maquette for Warrior
with Shield, 1952–53*

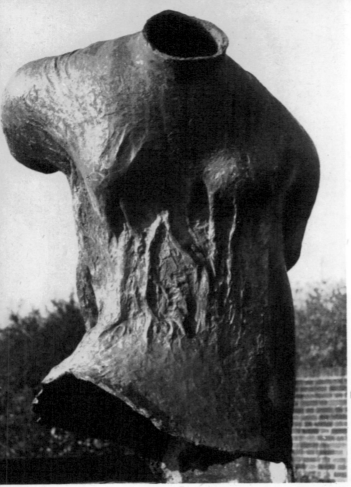

181 Draped Torso, 1953

From the same Greek inspiration the *Warrior with Shield (Pl. 178)* may have come. There is a bronze maquette for this figure *(Pl. 180)* and a large-scale *Warrior's Head* in bronze *(Pl. 179)*, the latter having a re-entrant cleft instead of a nose and a mouth indicated by a cross traversed by parallel lines which may not have any symbolic significance.

There remains from this period a work of very different character —the *Screen* carved for the Bond Street façade of the Time Life Building in London *(Pl. 184)*. Behind the screen, on a terrace not visible from the street, is a *Draped Reclining Figure (Pl. 182)* which is the familiar archetypal motive in its original configuration, the torso resting on retracted elbows, the knees drawn up parallel to each other. The only novelty is the drapery which clings to the body in close folds, suggesting a diaphanous material. This treatment of the drapery may also have been suggested by the sculpture Moore saw when he was in Greece the previous year, though the Elgin Marbles in the British Museum are a nearer source of inspiration. The figure looks caged-in in its present position on the terrace of the Time Life building, but there is a replica in a more appropriate setting in the inner court of the museum of the city of Cologne. Moore also cast an impressive *Draped Torso* in bronze *(Pl. 181)*, which is a study for the *Draped Reclining Figure*.

182 Draped Reclining Figure, 1952–53

It will have been noticed that most of the post-war works produced by Moore are basically naturalistic; however fantastic in detail they all reveal the sculptor's familiarity with the plastic values of the human body. This had led to the general impression already mentioned that by 1950 the sculptor had finally renounced his surrealistic tendencies, and certainly anything in the nature of abstraction. The Time Life *Screen* was a rude shock to all those people whose wish had fathered this thought. The four panels were original-ly conceived as figures revolving each in its frame—an idea abandoned for reasons of public safety (the public authority concerned thought they might come loose in their bearings and crash on to the heads of passers-by). They are all based on the human figure, but as in the

183 Unit of Time Life Screen, 1952

184 Time Life Screen, 1952–53

Square Form of 1936 *(Pl. 72)* already discussed, the various elements of the human body are 'squared-off' to fit into the predetermined opening in the screen. This is best seen in a detailed photograph of one of the units *(Pl. 183)*. Each of the geometrical forms corresponds to an element in the human body, but the general effect, determined by the necessity of having to make the screen conform to the dull geometrical façade of the building, is abstract. The building is not worthy of the screen, and its placing in a comparatively narrow street means that it is impossible to view the design from an appropriate distance. But it is significant in that it shows a modern sculptor trying to integrate his sculptural conception with architecture in direct cooperation with a modern architect. If the result is not completely satisfactory it is because the scale and situation and functional design of the building are not appropriate for sculpture: it is impossible to assimilate the essentially free art of sculpture to the strictly functional needs of modern architecture. Such assimilation was possible in the past (in the Greek temple and the Gothic cathedral) because architect and sculptor were inspired by identical artistic ideals.

199

CHAPTER NINE

The Works: Sixth Period 1955–64

To divide an artist's work, which is a continuous process, into periods is a convenience, but it becomes more and more arbitrary as his creative energy gathers confidence and momentum. The period of ten years which I propose to survey in this chapter will bring the story of Henry Moore's development up to the present time. It contains an unusual number of large important works, the minor works being for the most part studies for these major works. Certain motives persist from the past—the mother and child, the reclining figure, the helmet heads. The innovations are for the most part explorations of the human form and animal forms, and though they are often incorporated as variable details in the major works, these works themselves are all archetypal figures or groups animated by the same unconscious forces that throughout his career have led the sculptor to isolate and intensify two or three significant forms.

Apart from two or three smaller figures which repeat motives like the *Seated Girl* or *Mother and Child*, and a very original *Head: Lines (Pl. 185)* which seems to take up and develop the linear motives on a *Relief* of 1952 *(Pl. 162)*, and the similar lines on the *Leaf Figures* of the same year *(Pl. 161)*, but with a completely new intention (raised contours which define the masses and then sink into the central orifice), the maquettes of this year all lead up to the large wall relief commissioned by the Bouwcentrum in Rotterdam *(Pl. 187)*. This relief is carried out in brick—it is in fact a brick wall, 28¼ ft. high and 63 ft. long. The design consists of a central panel of brick, from which four figurative motives protrude, flanked by linear motives which are also designed in brickwork. A comparison of the finished wall with the maquette *(Pl. 186)* shows that the wall is a close reproduction of the sculptor's original conception, and apart from anything else, it is an interesting demonstration of the collaboration of the artist and the workman. Apart from minor trimmings, the whole design was carried out by the bricklayers. It represents an important extension of sculptural technique. It is true that brick sculpture is no innovation. There are examples of the technique in the Buddhist temples of Ceylon, especially the gigantic Buddha in the Lankatilaka shrine at Polonnaruva. More significant is the tradition of decorative brickwork in the Gothic churches of North Germany, a tradition which spread to Holland in the seventeenth century. Moore was therefore conforming to or reviving an indigenous art of Northern Europe, but his achievement at the Bouwcentrum was to use this traditional craft as a medium for his own informal images. In so far as his motives are linear they are not open to criticism: bricklaying is essentially a linear craft. As for the main plastic motives, brick as a fired clay is an appropriate medium for forms conceived in plaster, and the carving of what is in effect an artificial stone is strictly comparable to the carving of a natural stone—both kinds of stone have been fused by identical forces, one in the remote past, the other in the present day.

The motives themselves are anticipated by the *Relief* of 1952 *(Pl. 162)*, the *Corner Sculptures* of the same year *(Pl. 172)*, by the

186 *Wall Relief: Maquette No 1, 1955*

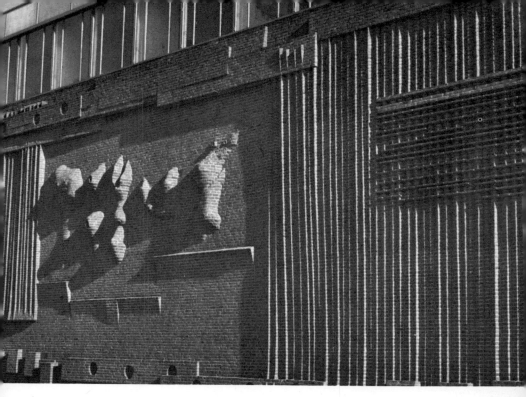

187 Wall Relief at Bouwcentrum, Rotterdam, 1955

Three Standing Figures of 1953 *(Pl. 157)*, by the first maquettes for the Time Life Screen (LH II, 64, 65), and by a curious object not so far mentioned, the *Bird Table* of 1954 (LH II, 84). The unusual number of motives elaborated on the maquettes (at least sixty can be counted) make this project a repertory of forms from which much subsequent plundering was possible. As for the nature of these motives, some are obviously based on the human figure, others on bone or shell formations, others (the most original) are a fusion of several motives into an upright form which might be compared with a totem-pole *(Pl. 188)*. Others seem to reproduce screws and metal strips *(Pl. 189)*.

Indeed, the next step was to extract from these maquettes a series of eleven small *Upright Motives*, some of which were then cast in bronze. Five of these were then enlarged, three to a monumental scale soaring to 126 inches *(Pl. 190)* and 132 inches *(Pl. 191)*. The

188 *Wall Relief: Maquette No 2, 1955*

189 *Wall Relief: Maquette No 3, 1955*

*190 Upright Motive
No 7, 1955–56*

highest has been called the Glenkiln Cross, from the position it occupies on Mr Keswick's estate in Scotland (there are altogether six replicas of this piece, one being in the Folkwang Museum, Essen, others at Hanover; Kröller-Müller Museum, Otterlo; Hirshhorn Collection, USA). The comparison with the totem-pole, though it has some superficial justification, is really misleading. The significance of totems varies from culture to culture and even from tribe to tribe, but generally speaking they have a precise function, i.e., to represent a particular animal (or plant) with which a man's or a tribe's ancestors were indivisibly linked in remote times. It is possible that the polés are also a phallic symbol, but this is certainly not their primary function.

The *Upright Motives* are based essentially on the human (female) body. In some of the versions the head and stunted arms form a cross, and this perhaps gives us a better clue to their significance. They remind me of the various 'crosses' which still stand in lonely places on the Yorkshire Moors—at least one of them, 'Fat Betty', is identified with the female body. The significance of these crosses is not known, but they are not necessarily Christian monuments. There are also the circles of upright stones near Kendal in Westmorland and at Avebury in Wiltshire, as well as the famous circle at Stonehenge and the prehistoric monoliths in Brittany (Carnac). None of these prehistoric monoliths is representational; their original purpose was no doubt in most cases ritualistic, and they still retain a super-real and uncanny significance for some people today.

However, these are historical rather than artistic prototypes; the formal origins and psychological significance of the Glenkiln Cross and other *Upright Motives* lie within the gradual unfolding of Moore's own archetypal vision. The *Upright Motives* might almost be regarded as a synthesis of the significant forms that had been realized in the previous twenty years of the sculptor's development—indeed, of the revolutionary conception of sculpture that was first evident in the *Composition* of 1931 *(Pl. 59)*. The 'head' of the Glenkiln Cross has the same blunted Cyclopic form as the *Composition* in carved concrete of 1933 belonging to the British Council *(Pl. 86)* or the Corsehill stone *Figure* of 1933–34 *(Pl. 88)*. The *Internal and External Forms*

H.MOORE

of 1953–54 *(Pl. 166)* anticipates the 'uprightness' of the motive, but it was on the first maquettes for the Rotterdam *Wall Relief (Pls. 186, 188, 189)* that all these elements from the past were assembled and 'tried out'. The final synthesis, however, is something more than the sum of all these 'ideas'; realized on a monumental scale (the Glenkiln Cross is 132 inches high) these 'motives' (an inadequate word to describe them) are apparitions of almost terrifying power. This power, I would say, is part libidinal part chthonic—some fusion of the immediately libidinal or erotic instincts and those 'archaic heritages', as Freud called them, that disturb the artist's consciousness with tantalizing recollections of past racial experiences, 'the forms of things unknown'. These are primordial images projected from the deepest level of the unconscious, and they illustrate the truth that the artist is essentially the instrument of unconscious forces. 'For art is innate in the artist, like an instinct that seizes and makes a tool out of the human being. The thing that in the final analysis wills something in him is not he, the personal man, but the aim of art. As a person he may have caprices and a will and his own aims, but as an artist he is in a higher sense "man", he is the *collective man*, the carrier and the shaper of the unconsciously active soul of mankind.'[1] These words of Jung may seem to remove art into the realm of mysticism, but they serve to explain, not only the artist's own inability to give a rational account of his work, but also the otherwise inexplicable power of that work over other people. Such power is an empirical fact, and we need an hypothesis like Jung's to explain it—the traditional aesthetics of beauty are inadequate.

We may now briefly review some smaller works before passing on to the next major piece, the UNESCO *Reclining Figure* of 1957–58. The *Falling Warrior* of 1956–57, *(Pl. 192)* is a variation of the *Warrior with Shield* of 1953–54 *(Pl. 178)*. A *Reclining Figure* of 1957 *(Pl. 196)* and a *Draped Reclining Figure* of 1957 *(Pl. 195)* are both variations of a familiar motive, but this motive received an unusual treatment in the large (108 inches) *Upright Figure* in elm wood of 1956–60 *(Pls. 193, 194)*. Apart from the fact that it is a return to direct carving, this figure shows a significant contrast to the Glenkiln Cross series. It is extremely sensuous in its realization of the female figure, but also shows the sculptor experimenting with the reclining figure as an upright motive—a contradiction of forms which is only realized by making the figure in effect a high relief—the base of the block of elm wood is left like a standing wall, and can only be effectively displayed as a relief. But the subsidiary elements in the figure are brought into harmony with this clinging posture—the head looks down, the buttocks hang like a pear, the legs flow into the ground. It is a significant piece because it shows how the sculptor is always conscious of the formal problems that arise from any shift in the body's position in relation to the law of gravity.

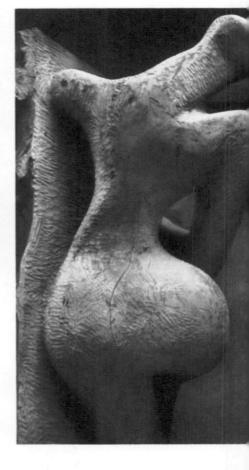

193 Upright Figure, 1956–60

194 Back view detail of Pl. 193

195 Draped Reclining Figure, 1957

196 Reclining Figure, 1957

We now come to one of the sculptor's greatest achievements, the *Reclining Figure* commissioned in 1956 for the Headquarters of UNESCO in Paris *(Pl. 199)*. As a member of the committee that was appointed by the Director General of UNESCO to advise on the works of art to be commissioned for the new building, I was intimately acquainted with the difficult problems that the artists had to solve. In designing their building the architects had made no provision for works of art and this created the greatest problem. There were no appropriate sites where works of art could function coherently— they could only be added as largely irrelevant décor. Picasso, Miró

197 Seated Figure against Curved Wall, 1956–57

198 *Two Seated Figures against Curved Wall, 1956–57*

and Moore were given the commissions for the largest works, and their difficulties were correspondingly most acute. In Moore's case he had to design a large piece of sculpture to be placed immediately in front of the main entrance façade of the building. This building, like most modern buildings, presented to the view a wide expanse of busy fenestration, and the architects had made the sculptor's task all the more difficult by adding to the façade a large porch with active wing-like outlines.

Moore therefore had to solve two problems—one, which was reminiscent of the Northampton commission, was to create a figure or group that had some relevance to its site—the headquarters of an international institution devoted to the diffusion of culture. The second problem was to accommodate such a figure or group against the 'busy' façade of the building.

199 *(pp. 214–15) UNESCO Reclining Figure, 1957–58*

Moore's first 'idea' was a female figure reading a book, or teaching a group of children, or just 'lost in contemplation', but the sculptural impact of such figures would be entirely obliterated by the background. He therefore tried out the possibility of placing the figures against a screen, which would be an integral part of the group *(Pls. 197, 198)*. This was to prove a fertile invention for the future, but it did not seem that it would 'work' in relation to the façade behind it. Finally, after much deliberation and discussion, Moore

200 Girl Seated against Square Wall, 1957–58

201 Armless Seated Figure against Round Wall, 1957

decided to revert to his familiar prototype, the Reclining Figure, but
to make this so massive that it would 'tell' against its background.

Moore chose Roman travertine marble as his medium, which,
once he had made his working model, he decided to carve in rough
outline in the quarry near Rome. He spent a few weeks there and
then the marble, weighing several tons, was transported to Paris,
erected on the site, and then carved by Moore to its final form
(Pl. 199). This form, by comparison with preceding Reclining Figures,
is extremely simplified—indeed, it reverts in its general outline to the
prototypical *Reclining Figure* of 1929 *(Pl. 43)*, and is nearest to the elm
wood figure of 1935–36 in the Albright-Knox Art Gallery, Buffalo

(Pl. 111). It is, however, more massive than any of its predecessors, and the thrust of the subsidiary elements within the total mass gives a tremendous impression of power held in reserve—perhaps not an inappropriate symbol for an organization whose declared aim is to establish peace in the minds of men. The head has an air of alert expectancy, of intellectual curiosity.

Arising from the preliminary work on this difficult commission are a large number of Seated Figures which were to be cast in bronze

202 *The Wall: Background for Sculpture, 1962*

203 Three Motives against Wall No 1, 1958

at intervals during the next five years. In some of these a 'wall' is incorporated (e.g., *Pls. 200, 201*), and this motive (which we have seen
in drawings as early as 1936 and long before any thought of the
UNESCO problem) reaches an independent monumental scale in *The
Wall* of 1962 *(Pl. 202)*, a castellated mass 84 inches high and 100 inches
long; it is still designated as a 'background for sculpture'. The wall
also plays a decisive part in the overall composition of *Three Motives
against Wall* of 1958 *(Pl. 203)*.

Closely following the UNESCO project are a number of pieces in
which Moore returns to a more direct interpretation of the human

204 *Woman*, 1957–58

(female) body—the *Woman* of 1957–58 *(Pl. 204)*, the *Seated Woman* of 1957 *(Pl. 208)*, the *Draped Seated Woman* of 1957–58 *(Pl. 206)* and the *Draped Reclining Woman* of the same year *(Pls. 207, 209)* which may be compared with the *Draped Reclining Figure* of the Time Life Building of five years earlier *(Pl. 182)*. The elm wood *Reclining Figure* of 1959–64 *(Pl. 205)* is a variation in a different material of the UNESCO figure, but the strange rectangular feature that thrusts upwards between the torso and the lower limbs is a distortion of some significance for future developments (see page 226 below).

205 Reclining Figure, 1959–64

206 *Draped Seated Woman, 1957–58*

207 *Back view of Pl. 209*

208 Seated Woman,
1957

209
Reclining Woman,
1957–58

The *Relief No 1* of 1959 *(Pl. 210)* is essentially an enlargement to gigantic size (88 inches) of one of the motives in the maquettes for the Rotterdam *Wall Relief*, and belongs to the same world of forms as the Glenkiln Cross. The torso has been modified into a sinister mask, reminiscent of the *Goat's Head* of 1952 *(Pl. 171)*, and is associated with *Animal Head* of 1956 *(Pl. 211)* and an *Animal Form* of 1959 *(Pl. 212)*.

210 Relief No 1, 1959

211 *Animal Head, 1956*

212 *Animal Form, 1959*

213 *Two-Piece Reclining Figure No 1, 1959*

We now come to the first of a series of gigantic Reclining Figures, the distinguishing features of which are their disintegration into two or three 'pieces', and a much nearer approximation to rock, cliff or cave forms. The first of these is the *Two-Piece Reclining Figure No 1* of 1959 (76 inches) *(Pl. 213)*. The figure is modelled in plaster and then cast in bronze, and the rough markings of the scraped and chiselled plaster are taken up by the bronze, giving the figure a rugged appearance. The torso is still close to the human body, though the arms are amputated; but the lower limbs are scarcely recognizable as such, the upper leg flying off at a tangent in the shape of a curved flange. In profile it has a distinctly phallic shape. This piece again has been set in the open landscape at Shawhead, Dumfries.

Two-Piece Reclining Figure No 2 is still larger (102 inches) and more cliff-like in appearance *(Pl. 214)*. The lower limbs are bent at the knee and from one point of view they have a distinct resemblance to the cliffs at Étretat so often painted by Courbet and other French artists. The torso is pierced by a cave-like hole, which adds to the cliff-like appearance. The tool-marks are still more rugged.

214 Two-Piece Reclining Figure No 2, 1960

215–16 Reclining Figure
on Pedestal, 1959–60

217 *Two-Piece Reclining Figure No 3, 1961*

A smaller (51¼ inches) *Reclining Figure on Pedestal* comes next (1959-60, *Pls. 215-16*), as do three maquettes for the *Two-Piece Reclining Figure No 3* of 1961 *(Pl. 217)* and the *Two-Piece Reclining Figure No 4* of the same year (LH III, 135), and finally the *Three-Piece Reclining Figure No 1* of 1961-62 *(Pl. 218)*. All these figures increase the anfractuosity of the rock-like formations and are a logical development of the theme. As compared with the early reclining figures, which might be said to assimilate the human body to a gently eroded landscape, almost a pastoral landscape, these later reclining figures assimilate

218 *(pp. 230–31) Three-Piece Reclining Figure No 1, 1961–62*

the body (and it is always the female body) to a rugged, broken, one might even say a sadistic landscape of rocks. As we look at these monumental forms, we can almost hear

> the whine in the rigging,
> The menace and caress of wave that breaks on water,
> The distant note in the granite teeth,
> And the wailing warning from the approaching headland...[2]

The next version of the reclining figure was to be more harmonious—the *Three-Piece Reclining Figure No 2: Bridge Prop* of 1963 *(Pl. 219)*. In this figure the three component elements—head and

219 Three-Piece Reclining Figure No 2: Bridge Prop, 1963

220 *Large Torso: Arch, 1962–63*

221 Reclining Mother and Child, 1960–61

shoulders, torso, lower limbs—have been smoothed and given a graceful curvilinear rhythm; they rest on the pedestal like the arches of a bridge. The arch 'idea' had been explored in a preliminary piece, the *Large Torso: Arch* of 1962–63 *(Pl. 220)*, and it is indeed implicit in many reclining figures almost from the beginning—the immediately preceding example is the *Reclining Mother and Child* of 1960–61, in which the torso and limbs are assimilated to one wide space-embracing arch *(Pl. 221)*. An arch is also made by the *Reclining Figure on Pedestal* of 1960 *(Pls. 215, 216)*, and the pedestal itself, an integral part of the figure, is arched.

234

The *Two-Piece Reclining Figure No 5 (Pl. 222)*, carried out in 1963–64, returns to some of the formal ideas of the first reclining figure in this series, but the torso rises in erect detachment, united to the rest of the figure only by its rhythmical stresses. Some of these rhythms are separately developed in the *Three-Way Piece No 1 (Points)* and in *Three-Way Piece No 2 (Archer) (Pl. 227)*. Both of 1964, these are bronzes of great precision and power.

222 Two-Piece Reclining Figure No 5, 1963–64

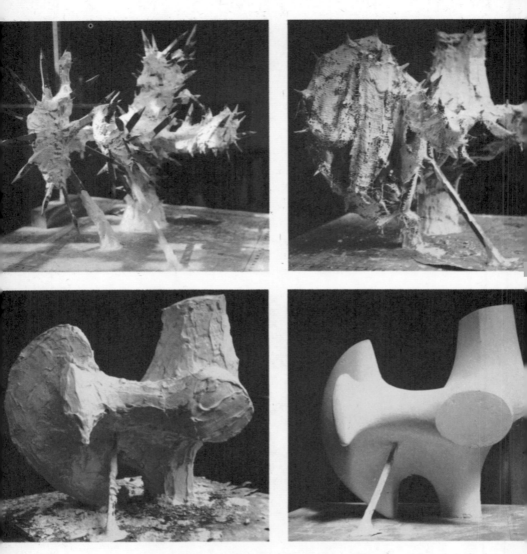

223–26 Progressive stages in the modelling of Three-Way Piece No 2 (Archer),
1964

227 *Three-Way Piece No 2 (Archer), 1964*

During the making and casting of these major pieces, Moore continued to produce a considerable number of minor pieces—minor only in the sense that they are smaller. *Two Seated Figures against Wall*, 1960 *(Pl. 198)* is a variation of the King and Queen group. The *Seated Woman with a Shell Skirt*, 1960 *(Pl. 228)*, a *Maquette for Seated Figure: Arms Outstretched (Pl. 230)*, the *Helmet Head No 3* (LH III, 155) the *Square Head* (LH III, 100)—all these of 1960—are works that display the sculptor's formal inventiveness and ability to develop an 'idea', but they do not differ essentially from works we have already discussed. The same may be said of the *Head: Cyclops* of 1962 (LH III, 156), and the *Helmet Head No 4* of 1963 *(Pl. 229)*. The *Three Part*

228 Seated Woman:

Shell Skirt, 1960

229 *Helmet Head No 4: Interior-Exterior, 1963*

Object (Pl. 231) and *Sculptural Object* (LH III, 104) both of 1960, are a return to what I have called biomorphic abstraction, and may be compared with much earlier pieces like the *Reclining Figure* in Hopton-wood stone of 1937 *(Pl. 93)* or even the clue piece to which I keep returning, the *Composition* of 1931 *(Pl. 59)*. Perhaps they are more nearly related to bones or shells rather than to the human figure, but there is always a suggestion of organic form.

230 Seated Figure: Arms Outstretched, 1960

A new motive is discovered in the *Seated Woman: Thin Neck* of 1961 *(Pl. 233)* and the *Standing Figure: Knife-Edge* of the same year *(Pl. 232)*. Here again are suggestions of bone and shell formations, but the real significance of these figures is the sculptor's ability to represent volume by means of the bone-like structure—just as certain

233 Seated Woman: Thin Neck, 1961

232 Standing Figure: Knife-Edge, 1961

scientists (palaeontologists) can reconstruct the form of an extinct animal on the evidence of one bone. The edge itself, of course, is a form that has a suggestion of dynamic force. It is carried to a fine perfection in the *Knife-edge: Two-Piece* of 1962, a highly polished bronze 28 inches high *(Pl. 235)*. The *Moon Head*, a bronze of 1964 *(Pl. 234)*, and the *Divided Head* of 1963 (LH III, 153) are further extensions of the knife-edge theme.

234 Moon Head, 1964

235 *Knife-Edge: Two-Piece, 1962*

And so we reach the last three pieces I propose to discuss. The first of them is the *Locking Piece* of 1963–64 *(Pl. 236)*. This is once again a new formal invention. It is foreshadowed in the Bridge Prop *Reclining Figure (Pl. 219)* in so far as the arched curvilinear components of that piece have some formal resemblance to the pieces that are interlocked in the *Locking Piece*, and there is a suggestion in the new piece that two segments of limbs have been joined together, rather in the manner that two bones interlock in the human groin or knee. The forms are complex and yet they seem to interlock with the perfection of a puzzle, and there is the same idea of the inevitability of one, and only one, solution. But the essential idea is perhaps one which Moore has often had in mind as a symbol of sculptural form: the clenched fist, the knuckles pale and glossy with an inherent striking-power.

The last piece to be completed by Moore at the time of writing is the *Atom Piece* of July, 1964 *(Pls. 237–38)*. The configuration of the piece was suggested by the shape of the cloud that rises after the explosion of an atom bomb—a beautiful shape, as is often the case with shapes associated with evil or murderous purposes—the shapes of spears, axes, swords, etc. This paradox, in which good and evil, beauty and power, unite in one symbol, is fully realized in this unusual piece—unusual because, if I am not mistaken, it is the only piece of sculpture by Henry Moore that is inspired by mechanical forces rather than organic growth. There is mechanical force in the forms of growth, as D'Arcy Thompson so wonderfully demonstrated[3], but normally the artist has most sympathy for the forms assumed by living organisms—organic form—a fact which has been fully demonstrated in the course of Henry Moore's whole development. Even in this case the dense dome-like cloud develops into a form similar to the compact bone-structure of the human skull, as if the sculptor were fully aware of this significant correspondence. The lower half of the sculpture is architectural, a series of arched cavities merging into a domed space reminiscent of the inside of a cathedral. The whole concept suggests the containment of a powerful force, in the way that a compact skull holds a brain capable of the wildest fantasies. The *Atom Piece* symbolizes those forces which

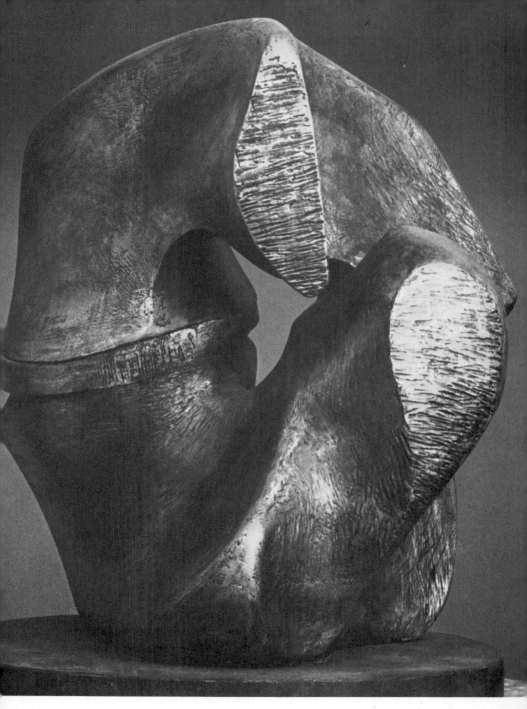

236 *Locking Piece, 1963–64*

237 *Atom Piece, 1964*

modern man has released for ends which cannot yet be imagined
or realized, but which for the present we inevitably associate with
universal destruction. At the same time it negates this evil intention
and returns the contemplating mind to a mood of stillness and serenity.

238 *Another view of Pl. 237*

The monumental group that was unveiled in October 1965 as the central feature of the plaza of the Lincoln Art Center in New York (*Pls. 239, 240*), will bring to an appropriate but provisional conclusion this survey of Moore's development as a sculptor. This piece is the extreme evolution of those variations of the reclining figure motive in which the extended limbs are magnified until they form a massive cliff-like extension, pierced by an arch. The torso rises against this rocky mass with a volcanic violence, in which, however, some element of the eternal feminine still confronts the general sense of of the earth's indifference. Set in water, this impassive monument is reflected against the changing moods of the overreaching sky. The Great Mother, the Goddess of Fertility, life itself as a tender force, broods over the desolate altars of a Waste Land. The creative genius of our artist has finally led us to a supreme symbol of our human destiny.

239 Working Model for Reclining Figure, Lincoln Center Sculpture, 1963–65

240 *Working Model for Reclining Figure, Lincoln Center Sculpture, 1963–65*

241   Reclining Figure, Lincoln Center Sculpture, 1963–65

CHAPTER TEN

Henry Moore's Achievement

Already in 1934, in the 'appreciation' that formed the text of the first book to be published on Henry Moore, I could write in a strain which is perhaps more appropriate to the present moment, thirty years later. 'Like all great artists', I concluded, 'he is consumed by an endless curiosity—curiosity concerning the possibilities of his materials, curiosity concerning the nature of life. That type of mind must necessarily explore a certain number of blind alleys, must discard some of its findings. The matter for wonder, in his case, is the consistency of his course, the gathering power, the increasing clearness of his intention. The life of an original artist of any kind—painter, sculptor, poet or musician—is hard; only an unfailing integrity of purpose can carry him through those years of financial failure, of public neglect or derision, which are his inevitable lot. All but a few are compelled to compromise. There has been no compromise in the life of Henry Moore, and now, in the fulness of his powers, he offers us the perfected product of his genius.'

His powers at that time had not reached their fulness nor had his work the perfection it now possesses, if by perfection we mean a completeness of realization of the artist's intentions. I was expressing my faith or conviction rather than a judgement based on adequate evidence. By now, however, the evidence is plentiful, and though Moore is still in the full flood of his creative powers, it is not likely that a considered appreciation of his work based on the existing body of his work will be seriously affected by either the quantity or the originality of what is still to come.

There are perhaps three main criteria for estimating the achievement of any great artist. The first is the fertility of his genius, though this is not in itself a sufficient test—there have been great artists who, by reason of their short lives, or even by reason of their unproductiveness, have left us with relatively little evidence of their genius—Giorgione, Fabritius and Vermeer are obvious examples. But the great artist is usually a prolific artist, and only a few sculptors in the history of European art have been as productive as Henry Moore.

Quantity in itself is no proof of genius, and the history of art again is a melancholy witness to the fact. The most absolute of all the criteria of greatness in art is the aesthetic one—the artist's ability to use his chosen medium with an absolute mastery of appropriate form. Moore's sense of form is absolute in this sense. I have given evidence from the artist's childhood which tends to prove that this sense is innate—it is a physical or nervous endowment, like absolute pitch in the apprehension of sound. But a physical endowment must

242 Outside the garden studio, Much Hadham

be nourished—in the case of a sculptor by visual and haptic experiences, and by technical training. The technical training is perhaps a routine affair, and does not differ essentially in any craft—painting, pottery or even bricklaying. Certainly there is nothing to distinguish the sculptor and the stonemason in this respect. But it is a necessary preliminary to that other aspect of training or education, which is concerned with the realization of the model.

A sensuous appreciation of form may be a natural endowment, but to *realize* one's sensations, as Cézanne used to say, is the great problem. How does the artist effect a correspondence between his sensations in front of the subject or motive and the form that emerges as he manipulates the material of his choice?

Again we must suppose that it is largely a question of natural endowment. The artist is measuring one sensation against another—what psychologists call the efferent sensation against the afferent sensation: his skill consists in the accurate balancing of these two kinds of sensation.

Moore has a perfected skill in this sense. How much it is the result of his close study of the human body and other natural forms, how much a development of his sense of the expressive potentialities of his chosen material, is impossible to estimate. Skill is a persistent application of the senses in the pursuit of an ideal form, and self-discipline, physical endurance, attention to detail, concentration of intuitive powers—all these intangible factors contribute to the final result. Again this is a characteristic of all great artists—what we call 'sheer horse-power', which is a question not only of concentrated will, but also of physical and nervous capability.

The third criterion of greatness is the one that is most difficult for a contemporary critic to estimate—the quality that Emerson used to write about—representativeness. By this we mean, not merely the social relevance of an artist's work, without which he is unlikely to gain the appreciation of his fellow-men during his lifetime, but rather the possession and projection into his work of certain insights which are universal. 'Sculpture may serve to teach the pupil how deep is the secret of form, how purely the spirit can translate its meanings into that eloquent dialect.'[1]

243 *Casting. The garden studio, Much Hadham*

The social relevance of Henry Moore's work, in an age that has invented the doctrine of socialist realism, has sometimes been questioned, but only by people who are either blinded by political prejudice or insensitive to significant form. It did not really need the occasion of war and the making of the Shelter Drawings to reveal Moore's humanity; that quality has been present in his work from the beginning. Only a humanist, a man concerned for the human condition, could have drawn the early life studies; only a humanist could have conceived and carved the Northampton *Madonna and Child*, or the many subsequent family groups and reclining figures. In all his work Moore is not only a humanist, in the sense that his work is intimately related to the human figure; but also in the wider sense of a man who has an acute awareness of the vital process itself, a feeling for organic form whether manifested in man, or animals, trees, plants, shells, fossils—whatever has been formed by the life-force in its endless procreative process.

If Moore had been satisfied with such traditional humanism he would not have advanced the art of sculpture beyond the point where it was left by Rodin and Maillol. But in conformity with other great artists of our time—Picasso and Klee above all—he has dared to seek below the level of consciousness for those archetypal forms that represent life in its deepest recesses and most powerful manifestations. The real distinction of the modern movement in art, a distinction which completely separates it from the Graeco-Roman and Renaissance tradition, lies in this new revelation. The modern artist has dared—and no one has been more explicit than Moore about his intentions in this respect—to abandon the ideal of beauty and establish in its place the ideal of vitality. But vitality is but a provisional word which serves to disguise the fact that we do not know and cannot measure the nature of life. Beauty is no mystery: it can be represented by geometrical formulas, by calculated proportions. But the vital process is intangible, and can be represented only by symbolic forms—forms symbolic of the essential nature of living organisms and forms symbolic of the racial experiences that have left an impress on our mental constitution—the archetypal patterns of birth and death, of social conflict and tragic drama.

244 *Henry Moore and Three-Piece Reclining Figure No 1*

Such archetypes were, of course, represented in the art of the past, and we have seen how Moore's archetypal motives, the Reclining Figure, the Mother and Child, the King and Queen, are echoes of the most powerful creations of the art of earlier ages. Some of these works, in prehistoric art, in tribal art, in the art of Sumer or Egypt, do not differ in their essential forms from Henry Moore's archetypal figures, and from this point of view it could be maintained that Moore is more traditional than the average academic artist. His originality does not lie in his motives, nor even in the aesthetic significance of his forms—in these respects he is a traditionalist. His originality is rather a consequence of his having extended the whole concept of tradition—of having reforged the links in the Great Chain of Being that had been broken by a materialistic conception of life and art.

This achievement has, I hope, been adequately described in my analysis of Moore's artistic development, but I would like to emphasize once again the unprogrammatic, the almost naive, nature of the process. Critics may interpret his achievement against the background of their knowledge of the history of art, of the science of art, of human psychology and social history; but the artist himself is not a scientist, a psychologist or an historian. He is a maker of images—or, as I prefer to call them because they have material existence—of icons, and he is impelled to make these icons by his sense of the forms that are vital to the life of mankind.

245 *Henry Moore with plaster version of Two-Piece Reclining Figure, No. 5*

Text References

Part One

ORIGINS AND EARLY ENVIRONMENT

1 (p. 15). Lorenzo Padgett, *Castleford & District in the Olden Time*, London and Castleford, 1904.

2 (p. 20). From a letter to the author.

EDUCATION THROUGH ART

1 (p. 31). Sir Michael Sadler was an authority on African art. He edited, and contributed a scholarly essay on 'The Significance and Vitality of African Art' to a volume on *Arts of West Africa*, published for the International Institute of African Languages and Cultures by the Oxford University Press in 1935.

2 (p. 33). *Vision and Design*. The Phoenix Library edition, 1928, p. 38. I quote the sentence as printed, but its grammatical structure is imperfect.

3 (p. 33). A new edition was published by the Marvell Press, Hessle, East Yorkshire, in 1960.

4 (p. 34). *Op. cit.*, p. 31.

5 (p. 35). In his *Recollections* (vol. 3, *Since Fifty*, London, 1939, p. 38) Rothenstein says that 'the two worked admirably together until Cole retired', but this is not the recollection of Henry Moore!

Part Two

THE WORKS: FIRST PERIOD 1921–25

1 (p. 51). *The Graphic*, 14 February, 1920.

2 (p. 52). Illustrated in *Gaudier-Brzeska* by Ezra Pound, *op. cit.* p. 33 above.

3 (p. 56). Victor Löwenfeld, *The Nature of Creative Activity*, Kegan Paul, London, 1939. The most accessible account of non-visual sources of drawing, painting and sculpture.

THE WORKS: SECOND PERIOD 1926–30

1 (p. 65). Vol. XXV, No. 641, pp. 598–9. Reprinted in *Sculpture and Drawings*, vol. 1, pp. xxxvi–xxxvii.

2 (p. 66). *The Archetypal World of Henry Moore*. New York (Bollingen Series), 1959.

THE WORKS: THIRD PERIOD 1931–36

1 (p. 83). C.f. my article, 'A Nest of Gentle Artists', in *Apollo*, September, 1962, reproduced in the catalogue of the exhibition of 'British Art in the "Thirties"', Marlborough Gallery, London, March 1965.

2 (p. 84). The best available illustrations are to be found in *Aegean Art* by Pierre Demargne, Thames and Hudson, London, 1964.

3 (p. 85). Alfred H. Barr, Jr., *Picasso: Fifty years of his Art*, Museum of Modern Art, New York, 1946, p. 150.

4 (p. 112). *Op. cit.*, pp. 99–100.

5 (p. 113). Henri Focillon, *The Life of Forms in Art*. Trans. Hogan and Kubler. Wittenborn, New York, 1948, p. 33.

THE WORKS: FOURTH PERIOD, DRAWINGS 1936–45

1 (p. 137). Reprinted in *Sculpture and Drawings*, vol. 1, pp. xxiii–xxxv.

THE WORKS: FIFTH PERIOD 1943–54

1 (p. 152). I have discussed this problem as it was first solved by the sculptors of the Renaissance in chapter three ('The Discovery of Space') of *The Art of Sculpture*, New York and London, 1956.

2 (p. 156). For a complete and profound discussion of this subject see *Sacred and Profane Beauty: the Holy in Art* by Gerardus van der Leeuw. Trans. David E. Green. New York, 1963. This sentence is quoted from p. 337.

3 (p. 176). *Op. cit.*, p. 117.

4 (p. 186). *Op. cit.*, p. 128.

THE WORKS: SIXTH PERIOD 1955–64

1 (p. 208). 'Psychology and Poetry' by C. G. Jung. *Collected Works*, vol. 15. Bollingen Foundation, New York and Routledge & Kegan Paul, London.

2 (p. 232). T. S. Eliot, 'The Dry Salvages', *The Four Quartets*, London (Faber), 1944.

3 (p. 246). *On Growth and Form*. Cambridge University Press, new edition, 1942.

HENRY MOORE'S ACHIEVEMENT

1 (p. 255). Emerson, Essay on 'Art' in *Essays*, London, 1883.

Select Bibliography

A detailed bibliography will be found in the three volumes of *Henry Moore, Sculpture and Drawings*, listed below. The present list is confined to books devoted entirely to Moore's works, and to general surveys which include items of documentary or critical interest.

Statements by Moore

The main statements made by Moore from time to time are included in the three volumes published by Lund Humphries (see READ, 1957, 1955, 1965). All his statements, writings, broadcasts and interviews, are to be collected in a volume edited by Philip James.

Books on Moore

READ, HERBERT: *Henry Moore, Sculpture and Drawings*. Vol. I, (1921–1948) fourth edn. 1957, edited by David Sylvester. London, Percy Lund, Humphries & Co., A. Zwemmer, xliii + 278 pp. illus.
Vol. II (since 1948). 1955. The same publisher, xxiv + 140 pp. illus.
Vol. III (1955–64). 1965. The same publisher. 32 pp + 179 pp. illus.

READ, HERBERT: *Henry Moore: Sculptor*. London, A. Zwemmer, 1934. 16 pp. + 36 pl.

NEUMANN, ERICH: *The Archetypal World of Henry Moore*. New York (Bollingen Series LXVIII), Pantheon Books, 1959. Trans. R.F.C. Hull. xv + 138 pp. illus.

GROHMANN, WILL: *The Art of Henry Moore*. London, Thames & Hudson Ltd., 1960.

Other books, catalogues, etc.

ARTS COUNCIL OF GREAT BRITAIN: *Sculpture and Drawings by Henry Moore*, at the Tate Gallery, London, 1951, 20 pp. + 44 pls. Catalogue prepared by A. D. B. Sylvester on the occasion of the Festival of Britain, May 2–July 29

GIEDION-WELCKER, CAROLA: *Contemporary Sculpture*. Revised edn., 1961 xxxi + 397 pp., illus. London (Faber & Faber); New York (Geo. Wittenborn, Inc.)

NEW YORK, MUSEUM OF MODERN ART: *Henry Moore*, by James Johnson Sweeney, 95 pp. illus. 1946. Exhibition monograph. Bibliography by H. B. Muller

SYLVESTER, A. D. B.: 'The Evolution of Henry Moore's Sculpture' *Burlington Magazine*, Vol. XC, London, July 1948. pp. 158–65, 189–95, illus.

READ, HERBERT: *A Letter to a Young Painter*. London, Thames and Hudson, 1962, pp. 151–71

READ, HERBERT: *A Concise History of Modern Sculpture*. London, Thames and Hudson, 1964

READ, HERBERT: *The Art of Sculpture*. New York, Bollingen Series, XXX, 3 (Pantheon Books) 2nd edn., 1961. London, Faber & Faber

READ, HERBERT: *The Philosophy of Modern Art*. London, Faber & Faber, 1952; New York (Horizon Press) 1953, pp. 195–215

List of Illustrations

When a single measurement is given, this indicates the longest dimension of the work in question. When two measurements are given, as in the case of drawings and reliefs, the height precedes the length. Photograph credits to the illustrations in Part One are given individually when known. All photographs in Part Two, unless otherwise stated, have been taken by the artist himself.

267

40 Reclining Woman, 1927
Cast concrete. L. 25 in
Collection Miss Mary Moore,
Much Hadham

41 Reclining Woman, 1926
Bronze. L. 16 in
Destroyed

42 North Wind, 1928–29
Portland stone. L. 96 in
Underground Building,
St James's, London

43 Reclining Figure, 1929
Brown Hornton stone. L. 33 in
Collection Leeds City Art Gallery

44 Reclining Figure, 1929
Alabaster. L. 18³/₈ in
Collection Marlborough Fine Art
Ltd., London

45 Reclining Woman, 1930
Green Hornton stone. L. 37 in
Collection National Gallery of
Canada, Ottawa

46 Reclining Figure, 1930
Ironstone. L. 7 in
Collection Robert J. Sainsbury,
London

47 Reclining Figure, 1930
Ancaster stone. L. 21 in
Collection Miss Lois Orswell,
Pomfret, Connecticut

48 Mask, 1929
Cast concrete. H. 8¹/₂ in
Collection Sir Philip Hendy,
London

49 Mask, 1929
Stone. H. 5 in
Collection Miss Mary Moore,
Much Hadham

50 Figure with clasped Hands, 1929
Travertine marble. H. 18 in
Collection Tel Aviv Museum

51 Seated Figure, 1930
Alabaster. H. 15 in
Collection A. J. McNeill Reid,
Scotland

52 Girl with clasped Hands, 1930
Cumberland alabaster. H. 15 in
Collection British Council,
London

53 Half-figure, 1930
Ancaster stone. H. 20 in
Collection National Gallery of
Victoria, Melbourne
Photo: E. J. Mason

54 Mother and Child, 1929
Verde di prato. H. 4³/₄ in
Collection Sir Kenneth Clark,
Saltwood

55 Mother and Child, 1929
Stone. H. 5 in
Private collection

56 Figure, 1930
Boxwood. H. 14 in
Private collection
Photo: Adolph Studly, New York

57 Torso, 1927
African wood. H. 15 in
Collection Marlborough Fine Art
Ltd., London
Photo: Marlborough Fine Art
Ltd., London

58 Figure, 1930
Ebony. H. 10 in
Collection Mrs Michael Ventris,
London

59 Composition, 1931
Green Hornton stone. H. 19 in
Collection Mrs Irina Moore,
Much Hadham

60 'Lyre Playing Idol'
Cycladic Period
Collection National Museum,
Athens

61 Pablo Picasso
Project for a Monument, 1928
Bronze. H. 8⁵/₈ in
Collection the artist
Photo: Brassaï, Paris

62 Relief, 1931
Plaster. H. 18¹/₄ in
Collection the artist
Photo: Errol Jackson

63 Reclining Figure, 1931
Lead. L. 17 in
Collection Mr and Mrs Frederick
Zimmerman, New York

64 Head and Ball, 1934
Cumberland alabaster. L. 20 in
Collection Harold Diamond,
New York

65 Bird and Egg, 1934
Cumberland alabaster. L. 22 in
Collection Harold Diamond,
New York

66 Three-Piece Carving, 1935
Ebony. L. 17 in
Originally carved in stone (1934)
and destroyed

67 Four-Piece Composition:
Reclining Figure, 1934
Cumberland alabaster. L. 20 in
Collection Miss Martha Jackson,
New York

68 Study for a Reclining Figure as a
Four-Piece Composition, 1934
Pen and watercolour. 22 × 15 in
Collection Sir Kenneth Clark,
Saltwood

69 Reclining Figure and Ideas for
Sculpture, c. 1933
Pen and wash. 22 × 15 in
Private collection

70 Composition, 1934
Reinforced concrete. L. 17¹/₂ in
Cast in bronze, 1961
Edition of 9
Private collections
Photo: John Hedgecoe, London

71 Carving, c. 1936
Travertine marble. H. 18 in
Collection the artist

72 Square Form, 1936
Green Hornton stone. L. 16 in
Collection Robert J. Sainsbury,
London

73 Abstract Drawing in colour, 1935
Pen and watercolour. 15 × 21³/₄ in
Collection Lady Norton, London

74 Square Form, 1936
Brown Hornton stone. L. 21 in
Collection Dr van der Wal,
Amsterdam

75 Carving, 1936
Brown Hornton stone. L. 20 in
Collection Martha Jackson
Gallery, New York

76 Two Stone Forms, 1936
Pen and wash. 22 × 15 in
Collection Sir Kenneth Clark,
Saltwood
Photo: John Webb, London

77 Two Forms, 1936
Hornton stone. H. 42 in
Collection Mrs H. Gates Lloyd,
Haverford, Pennsylvania

78 Stones in Landscape, 1936
Pen and wash. 22 × 15 in
Collection Mrs William F. C. Ohly

79 Mother and Child, 1936
Green Hornton stone. H. 45 in
Collection Roland Penrose,
Chidingly

80 Reclining Figure, 1932
Carved reinforced concrete.
L. 43 in
Collection City Art Museum,
St Louis

81 Mother and Child, 1931
Verdi di prato. H. 8 in
Collection Michael Maclagan,
Oxford

82 Carving, 1934
African Wonderstone. H. 4 in
Collection Miss Mary Moore,
Much Hadham

83 Girl, 1932
Boxwood. H. $12^1/_2$ in
Collection Mrs Barbara von
Bethmann-Hollweg, London

84 Mother and Child, 1932
Green Hornton stone. H. 35 in
Collection Robert J. Sainsbury,
London
Photo: Errol Jackson

85 Composition, 1932
Dark African wood. H. $15^1/_4$ in
Collection Sir Kenneth Clark,
Saltwood
Photo: John Webb, London

86 Composition, 1933
Carved concrete. H. 23 in
Collection British Council,
London

87 Figure, 1931
Beechwood. H. $9^1/_2$ in
Collection Tate Gallery, London

88 Figure, 1933–34
Corsehill stone. H. 30 in
Collection Marlborough Fine Art
Ltd., London

89 Composition, 1933
Walnut-wood. H. 14 in
Collection Douglas Glass,
London

90 Two Forms, 1934
Ironstone. H. $7^1/_4$ in
Collection Marlborough Fine Art
Ltd., London

91 Two Forms, 1934
Pynkado wood, oak base. L. 21 in
Collection Museum of Modern
Art, New York

92 Sculpture, 1937
Hopton-wood stone. L. 20 in
Collection Martha Jackson
Gallery, New York

93 Reclining Figure, 1937
Hopton-wood stone. L. 33 in
Collection Miss Lois Orswell,
Pomfret, Connecticut

94 Head, 1937
Hopton-wood stone. H. 21 in
Collection Martha Jackson
Gallery, New York

95 Figure, 1937
Bird's eye marble. H. 20 in
Collection Morton D. May,
St Louis

96 Stringed Relief, 1937
Beechwood and string. H. $19^1/_2$ in
Collection J. C. Pritchard, London

97 Stringed Figure, 1939
Lead and wire. L. 10 in
Collection Mrs Irina Moore,
Much Hadham
Also in bronze and string
(edition of 9)

98 The Bride, 1939–40
    Lead and wire. H. $9^3/_8$ in
    Collection Museum of Modern
    Art, New York
    Photo: The Garraway Company,
    Rutherford, N.J.

99 Stringed Figure, 1938
    Lignum vitae and string. H. 14 in
    Collection G. Burt, London

100 Bird Basket, 1939
    Lignum vitae and string.
    L. $16^1/_2$ in
    Collection Mrs Irina Moore,
    Much Hadham

101 Mother and Child, 1938
    Lead and wire. H. 5 in
    Collection Mrs Fanny Wadsworth,
    London

102 Reclining Figure, 1938
    Lead. L. 13 in
    Collection Museum of Modern
    Art, New York
    Also in bronze (edition of 3)
    Collections: Miss Peggy
    Guggenheim, Venice;
    and others

103 Reclining Figure, 1938
    Lead. L. $5^1/_2$ in
    Collection Rupert Doone, London

104 Bronze Cast of Interior Figure for
    Pl. 105
    Collection the artist

105 The Helmet, 1939–40
    Lead. H. 11 in
    Collection Roland Penrose,
    Chidingly
    Also in bronze

106 Reclining Figure, 1939
    Lead. L. 13 in
    Private collection
    Also in bronze

107 Pointed Forms, 1940
    Pencil, chalk, pen and watercolour.
    10 × 17 in
    Collection Mrs Irina Moore,
    Much Hadham
    Photo: British Council, London

108 Three Points, 1939–40
    Lead. L. $7^1/_2$ in
    Collection Mr and Mrs Alan Best,
    London
    Also in cast iron
    Collection Mrs Irina Moore,
    Much Hadham
    Also in bronze

109 Figure, 1939
    Lead. H. 16 in
    Collection Mrs Patricia Strauss,
    London

110 Drawing, 1938
    Chalk and watercolour. 15 × 22 in
    Private collection

111 Reclining Figure, 1935–36
    Elm wood. L. 35 in
    Collection Albright-Knox Art
    Gallery, Buffalo

112 Reclining Figure, 1936
    Elm wood. L. 42 in
    Collection Wakefield City Art
    Gallery and Museum

113 Recumbent Figure, 1938
    Green Hornton stone. L. 55 in
    Collection Tate Gallery, London
    Photo: Tate Gallery

114 Another view of Pl. 113

115 Reclining Figure, 1939
    Elm wood. L. 81 in
    Collection Detroit Institute of Art

116 Reclining and Seated Figures, 1931
Wash and watercolour. 22 × 15 in
Collection Paul Wengraf
Photo: British Council, London

117 Seated Figures, 1932
Drawing for sculpture
Chalk, pen and wash.
$14^3/_4$ × $10^3/_4$ in
Private collection

118 Reclining Figure, 1942
Chalk, pen, wash and watercolour.
17 × 22 in
Collection Sir Kenneth Clark,
Saltwood
Photo: John Webb, London

119 Crowd looking at a tied-up
Object, 1942
Chalk, pen, wash and watercolour.
17 × 22 in
Collection Sir Kenneth Clark,
Saltwood
Photo: John Webb, London

120 Figures in a Cave, 1936
Chalk and wash. 15 × 22 in
Private collection

121 Drawing for Metal Sculpture,
1937
Chalk and wash. 15 × 22 in
Collection the artist
Photo: John Webb, London

122 Drawing for Metal Sculpture, 1937
Chalk and watercolour. 15 × 22 in
Collection Sir Herbert Read,
Stonegrave

123 Two Women, 1939
Drawing for Sculpture combining
wood and metal.
Chalk and watercolour.
$17^1/_2$ × 15 in
Collection Sir Kenneth Clark,
Saltwood

124 Page from Shelter Sketchbook,
1941
Head of Sleeper
Chalk, pen and watercolour.
$8^1/_2$ × $6^1/_2$ in
Collection Mrs Irina Moore,
Much Hadham

125 Page from Shelter Sketchbook,
1941
Sleeping Positions
Chalk, pen and watercolour.
$8^1/_2$ × $6^1/_2$ in
Collection Mrs Irina Moore,
Much Hadham

126 Row of Sleepers, 1941
Wax, chalk, pen and watercolour.
21 × $12^5/_8$ in
Collection British Council,
London

127 Page from Shelter Sketchbook,
1941
Tube shelter perspective
Chalk, pen and watercolour.
$8^1/_2$ × $6^1/_2$ in
Collection Mrs Irina Moore,
Much Hadham

128 Studies of Miners at Work, 1942
Chalk, pen and watercolour.
22 × 17 in
Collection Whitworth Art Gallery
Manchester

129 The Family, 1944
Project for Sculpture. 24 × 19 in
Collection Sir Michael Balcon,
London

130 Family Groups, 1944
Chalk, pen and watercolour.
$19^1/_2$ × $12^1/_2$ in
Collection Miss Jill Craigie

131 Project for Relief Sculptures, 1938
Chalk, pen and wash.
14³/₄ × 10¹/₂ in
Collection Sir Philip Hendy,
London

132 Madonna and Child, 1943–44
In progress

133 Madonna and Child, 1943–44
In progress

134 Madonna and Child, 1943–44
Hornton stone. H. 59 in
Church of St Matthew,
Northampton

135 Family Group, 1944
Terracotta. H. 6¹/₈ in
Collection Miss Mary Moore,
Much Hadham
Also in bronze (edition of 7)
Private collections

136 Family Group, 1945
Bronze. H. 9¹/₂ in
Edition of 9
Private collections

137 Family Group, 1947
Bronze. H. 16 in
Edition of 7
Private collections

138 Detail of Pl. 139
Photo: Lidbrooke, London

139 Family Group, 1945 and 1949
Bronze. H. 60 in
Edition of 4
Collections: Barclay School,
Stevenage, Herts; Museum of
Modern Art, New York; Tate
Gallery, London; Nelson D.
Rockefeller, New York

140 Madonna and Child, 1943 and
1949
Hornton stone. H. 48 in
St Peter's Church, Claydon,
Suffolk

141 Madonna and Child, 1943
5 sketch-models in terracotta
Centre figure H. 7¹/₄ in; the other
four H. 5³/₄ in
Private collections

142 Reclining Figure, 1945
Bronze. L. 16 in
Edition of 7
Private collections

143 Reclining Figure, 1945
Bronze. L. 17¹/₂ in
Edition of 7
Private collections

144 Memorial Figure, 1945–46
Hornton stone. L. 56 in
Dartington Hall, Devon

145 Three Standing Figures, 1947–48
Darley Dale stone. H. 84 in
Battersea Park, London
(Gift of the Contemporary Art
Society)

146 Reclining Figure, 1945–46
In progress

147 Reclining Figure, 1945–46
In progress

148 Reclining Figure, 1945–46
Elm wood. L. 75 in
Collection Cranbrook Academy of
Art, Bloomfield Hills, Michigan

149 Reclining Figure, 1946–47
Brown Hornton stone L. 27 in
Collection Henry R. Hope,
Bloomington, Indiana

150 Standing Figure, 1950
Bronze. H. 87 in
Edition of 4
Collections: W. J. Keswick
Shawhead, Dumfries;
Dr van der Wal, Amsterdam

151 Standing Figures, 1948
Ideas for Metal Sculpture
Chalk and watercolour.
$11^1/_2 \times 9^1/_2$ in
Private collection, USA

152 Double Standing Figure, 1950
Bronze. H. 87 in
Edition of 2
Collections: S. J. Salter, New
York; Edgar Kauffman Sr.,
Pennsylvania

153 Family Group, 1951
Chalk and watercolour. 20 × 17 in
Collection R. Clarke, Christchurch,
New Zealand

154 Rocking Chair No 3, 1950
Bronze H. $12^1/_2$ in
Edition of 6
Private collections
(There is also a smaller version
6 in high)

155 Rocking Chair No 2, 1950
Bronze. H. 11 in
Edition of 6
Private collections

156 Mother and Child, 1953
Bronze. H. 20 in
Edition of 7
Private collections

157 Three Standing Figures, 1953
Bronze. H. 28 in
Edition of 6
Blanden Memorial Gallery, Iowa;
Private collections

158 Helmet Head No 2, 1950
Lead. H. $13^1/_2$ in
Collection Mrs Irina Moore,
Much Hadham
Also in bronze (edition of 9)
Private collections

159 Helmet Head and Shoulders, 1952
Bronze. H. $6^1/_2$ in
Edition of 10
Private collections
Photo: Louise van der Veen,
Amsterdam

160 Five Figures (interiors for lead
helmets), 1950
Lead. H. 5 in
Collection the artist

161 Leaf Figures Nos 1 and 2, 1952
Bronze. H. 10 in
Edition of 9
Private collections

162 Relief No 1, 1952
Bronze. H. $4^3/_4$ in
Edition of 7
Private collections

163 Reclining Figure No 5, 1952
Bronze. L. $8^1/_2$ in
Edition of 9
Private collections

164 Maquette for Upright Internal
and External Forms, 1951
Bronze. H. 7 in
Edition of 7
Private collections

165 Working Model for Upright
Internal and External Forms,
1951
Bronze. $24^1/_2$ in
Edition of 7
Collections: Rhode Island School
of Design, USA; Kunstmuseum,
Basle; Art Gallery of Toronto,
Canada; private collections

181 Draped Torso, 1953
Bronze. H. 35 in
Edition of 4
Collections: Mr and Mrs Stead-
Ellis, Stirlingshire; Sir Robert and
Lady Abdy, Cornwall; A. K. So-
lomon, Massachusetts; Ferens
Art Gallery, Hull

182 Draped Reclining Figure, 1952–53
Bronze. L. 62 in
Edition of 3
Time Life Building, London; City
of Cologne, Germany; Joseph H.
Hirshhorn, New York

183 Unit of Time Life Screen, 1952
Portland stone. H. 102 in

184 Time Life Screen, 1952–53
Portland stone. 120 × 318 in
Time Life Building, London

185 Head: Lines, 1955
Bronze. H. 11³/₄ in
Edition of 7
Private collections

186 Wall Relief: Maquette No 1, 1955
Bronze. 10 × 22¹/₂ in
Edition of 12
Private collections

187 Wall Relief at Bouwcentrum,
Rotterdam, 1955
Brick. 28¹/₆ × 63 ft
Commissioned in 1954 for the
façade of the Bouwcentrum
(Building Centre) in Rotterdam

188 Wall Relief: Maquette No 2, 1955
Bronze. 13 × 17¹/₂ in
Edition of 10
Private collections
Photo: Lidbrooke, London

189 Wall Relief: Maquette No 3, 1955
Bronze. 13 × 19 in
Edition of 10
Private collections
Photo: Lidbrooke, London

190 Upright Motive No 7, 1955–56
Bronze. H. 126 in
Edition of 5
Collections: Dr W. Stähelin,
Zürich; Amon Carter Museum,
Fort Worth, Texas; Kröller-Müller
Museum, Otterlo

191 Upright Motives No 7, No 1
(Glenkiln Cross) and No 2,
1955–56
Bronze. H. 126 in, 132 in, 126 in
Edition of 2
Collections: Kröller-Müller Mu-
seum, Otterlo; Amon Carter
Museum, Fort Worth, Texas
Photo: Bo Boustedt

192 Falling Warrior, 1956–57
Bronze. L. 58 in
Edition of 10
Collections: Joseph H. Hirshhorn,
New York; Very Reverend Walter
Hussey, Chichester; Maurice
Cooke, Bangor, Wales; Clare
College, Cambridge; Nathan
Cummings, Chicago; Mr and Mrs
Max Wasserman, Chestnut Hill,
Massachusetts; Walker Art Gall-
ery, Liverpool; Municipality of
Zollikon, Zürich; Glyptothek,
Munich; Huddersfield Art Gallery

193 Upright Figure, 1956–60
Elm wood. H. 108 in
Collection Solomon R. Guggen-
heim Museum, New York

194 Back View of Pl. 193

195 Draped Reclining Figure, 1957
Bronze. L. 29 in
Edition of 11
Private collections

196 Reclining Figure, 1957
Bronze. L. 27¹/₂ in
Edition of 12
Private collections

197 Seated Figure against Curved Wall
1956–57
Bronze. H. (figure) 18 in
Edition of 12
Collections: Arts Council of Great
Britain, London; Museum of Fine
Arts, Boston; National Gallery of
South Australia, Adelaide; private
collections

198 Two Seated Figures against
Curved Wall, 1956–57
Preliminary plaster maquette for
UNESCO Project. L. 11 in
Collection the artist
Photo: Lidbrooke, London

199 UNESCO Reclining Figure,
1957–58
Roman Travertine marble,
L. 200 in
Commissioned in 1956 for the
forecourt of the UNESCO
headquarters in Paris

200 Girl Seated against Square Wall,
1957–58
Bronze. H. (including wall) 40 in
Edition of 12
Private collections

201 Armless Seated Figure against
Round Wall, 1957
Bronze. H. (including wall) 11 in
Edition of 12
Collection Boston University;
private collections

202 The Wall: Background for Sculp-
ture, 1962
(Originally conceived as a back-
ground for *Standing Figure:
Knife-Edge, Pl. 232*)
Bronze. 84 × 100 in
Edition of 3

203 Three Motives against Wall No 1,
1958
Bronze. L. (wall) 42 in
H. (motives) 14 in
Edition of 12
Collections: Victoria and Albert
Museum, London; Museum of
Modern Art, New York; private
collections

204 Woman, 1957–58
Bronze. H. 60 in
Edition of 8
Collections: Museum des 20 Jahr-
hunderts, Vienna; Ted Weiner,
Fort Worth, Texas; Otto Pre-
minger, New York; Gustav Stein,
Cologne; Mr and Mrs Samuel
Zacks, Toronto; Arnold Mare-
mont, Chicago; British Council,
London

205 Reclining Figure, 1959–64
Elm wood. L. 90 in
Collection the artist

206 Draped Seated Woman, 1957–58
Bronze. H. 73 in
Edition of 6
Collections: City of Wuppertal,
Germany; London County Coun-
cil (Stifford Estate, Clive Street,
Stepney); Musées Royaux des
Beaux-Arts, Brussels; Yale Uni-
versity, New Haven, Connecticut;
National Gallery of Victoria, Mel-
bourne; Hebrew University, Jeru-
salem

207 Back view of Pl. 209

208 Seated Woman, 1957
Bronze. H. 57 in
Edition of 6
Collections: Lester Avnet, Great
Neck, New York; Mr and Mrs W.
R. Servaes, Surrey; Joseph H.
Hirshhorn, New York; David
Finn, New York; Dr Hans Neu-
mann, Caracas, Venezuela; Galerie
des 20 Jahrhunderts, Berlin

209 Draped Reclining Woman,
1957–58
Bronze. L. 82 in
Edition of 6
Collections: Dr W. Stähelin,
Zürich; Edward Albee, New
York; Neue Staatsgalerie,
Munich; Mr and Mrs R. J. Sains-
bury, Bucklebury, Berks; Gustav
Kahnweiler, Gerrards Cross,
Bucks; Federal Parliament, State
of Baden-Württemberg, Stuttgart

210 Relief No 1, 1959
Bronze. H. 88 in
Edition of 6
Opera House, Berlin

211 Animal Head, 1956
Bronze. L. 22 in
Edition of 10
Kröller-Müller Museum, Otterlo;
private collections

212 Animal Form, 1959
Bronze. H. 9³/₄ in
Edition of 8
Collection Zoological Society of
London (Stamford Raffles Award)

213 Two-Piece Reclining Figure No 1,
1959
Bronze. L. 76 in
Edition of 6
Collections: Lambert Airport,
St Louis; Lehmbruck Museum,
Duisburg; Chelsea School of Art,
London; Maurice Ash, Ash-
prington, Devon; Walter Carsen,
Don Mills, Ontario; Albright-
Knox Art Gallery, Buffalo

214 Two-Piece Reclining Figure No 2,
1960
Bronze. L. 102 in
Edition of 7
Collections: Lambert Airport,
St Louis; National Gallery of
Scotland, Edinburgh; Tate Gall-
ery, London; Kröller-Müller Mu-
seum, Otterlo; Museum of Mod-
ern Art, New York; Mr and Mrs
Milton Sperling, California

215 Reclining Figure on Pedestal,
1959–60
Bronze. H. 51¹/₄ in
Edition of 9
Collections: Gunnar Didrichsen,
Helsinki; Museo de Bellas Artes,
Caracas, Venezuela; private col-
lections

216 Another view of Pl. 215

217 Two-Piece Reclining Figure No 3,
1961
Bronze. L. 94 in
Edition of 7
Collections: Ted Weiner, Fort
Worth, Texas; SITOR, Turin;
City of Gothenburg, Sweden;
David Bright, Beverly Hills, Cali-
fornia; London County Council
(Brandon Estate, Southwark);
Museum of Fine Arts, Dallas,
Texas; Everson Museum of Art,
Syracuse

218 Three-Piece Reclining Figure
No 1, 1961–62
Bronze. L. 113 in
Edition of 7
Collections: National Bank of
Canada, Montreal; Bart Lytton,
Los Angeles; William H. Weint-
raub, New York

219 Three-Piece Reclining Figure
No 2: Bridge Prop, 1963
Bronze. L. 99 in
Edition of 6
Collections: City Art Gallery,
Leeds; Joseph H. Hirshhorn, New
York

220 Large Torso: Arch, 1962–63
Bronze. H. 78^1/$_2$ in
Edition of 6
Collections: Dr W. Stähelin,
Zürich; Museum of Modern Art,
New York

221 Reclining Mother and Child,
1960–61
Bronze. L. 86^1/$_2$ in
Edition of 7
Collections: Mr and Mrs Albert
List, New York; Carleton Byron
Swift, Washington DC; Walker
Art Center, Minneapolis; Taft
Schreiber, Beverly Hills, Cali-
fornia; Mrs Sara Hilden, Helsinki

222 Two-Piece Reclining Figure No 5,
1963–64
Bronze. L. 147 in
Edition of 2

223–26 Progressive stages in the
modelling of Three-Way Piece
No 2 (Archer), 1964

227 Three-Way Piece No 2 (Archer),
1964
Bronze. H. 30^1/$_2$ in
Edition of 7

228 Seated Woman: Shell Skirt, 1960
Bronze. H. 8^3/$_4$ in
Edition of 12
Private collections

229 Helmet Head No 4: Interior-
Exterior, 1963
Bronze. H. 18^3/$_4$ in
Edition of 6
Private collections

230 Seated Figure: Arms Outstretched,
1960
Bronze. H. 6^1/$_2$ in
Edition of 9
Private collections

231 Three Part Object, 1960
Bronze. H. 48^1/$_2$ in
Edition of 9
Private collections

232 Standing Figure: Knife-Edge,
1961
Bronze. H. 112 in
Edition of 7
Collections: Frank Stanton, New
York; Perini-San Francisco Asso-
ciates, Golden Gateway Project,
San Francisco; Bruce Dayton,
Minneapolis; City of Essen; MCA
Universal City, California; David
Lloyd Kreeger, Washington DC;
private collection

233 Seated Woman: Thin Neck, 1961
Bronze. H. 64 in
Edition of 7
Collections: Mr and Mrs Max
Wasserman, Chestnut Hill, Mas-
sachusetts; Skidmore, Owings
and Merrill, New York; Des
Moines Art Center, Iowa; Dr and
Mrs Aerol Arnold, Beverly Hills,
California; Laing Art Gallery,
Newcastle upon Tyne; Dr A.
Zaffaroni, Palo Alto, California;
Gordon Bunshaft, New York

234 Moon Head, 1964
Bronze. H. 22^1/$_2$ in
Edition of 9
Private collections

235 Knife-Edge: Two-Piece, 1962
Bronze. L. 28 in
Edition of 10
Collections: Tate Gallery, London; British Council, London; Arts Council of Great Britain, London; Kunsthaus, Zürich; Gemeente Museum, The Hague; Rochester University; private collections

236 Locking Piece, 1963–64
Bronze. H. 115 in
Edition of 3
Collection: Banque Lambert, Brussels

237 Atom Piece, 1964
Bronze. H. 48 in
Edition of 6
Private collections

238 Another view of Pl. 237

239 Reclining Figure, Lincoln Center Sculpture, 1963-65
Working Model
Bronze. L. 162 in, H. 93 in
Photo: Frank Stanton, New York

240 Another view of Pl. 239
Photo: Frank Stanton, New York

241 Reclining Figure, Lincoln Center Sculpture, 1963-65
Bronze. H. 19^1/$_2$ ft
Lincoln Center for the Performing Arts, New York
Photo: Marlborough Fine Art, Ltd., London

242 Outside the garden studio, Much Hadham
Photo: Crispin Eurich, London

243 Casting in the garden studio, Much Hadham
Photo: David Moore

244 Henry Moore and *Three-Piece Reclining Figure No 1*, 1961–62
Photo: J. S. Lewinski, London

245 Henry Moore and plaster version of *Two-Piece Reclining Figure No 5*
Photo: J. S. Lewinski, London

Index